T0001554

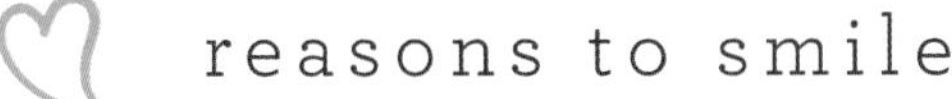
reasons to smile

Reasons to Smile

Celebrating People with Down Syndrome Around the World

Edited by Andrea Knauss & Elizabeth Martins
Foreword by Keith Harris

4880 Lower Valley Road • Atglen, PA 19310

Other Schiffer Books by the Author:
Reasons to Smile, ISBN 978-0-7643-5040-5

Library of Congress Control Number: 2022932092

Designed by Lori Butanis
Cover design by Danielle Farmer
"Welcome to Holland" © 1987 by Emily Perl Kingsley.
All rights reserved. Reprinted by permission of the author.
Type set in Archer and Amplitude

ISBN: 978-0-7643-6462-4
Printed in India

Published by Schiffer Publishing, Ltd.
4880 Lower Valley Road
Atglen, PA 19310
Phone: (610) 593-1777; Fax: (610) 593-2002
Email: Info@schifferbooks.com
Web: www.schifferbooks.com

For our complete selection of fine books on this and related subjects, please visit our website at www.schifferbooks.com. You may also write for a free catalog.

Schiffer Publishing's titles are available at special discounts for bulk purchases for sales promotions or premiums. Special editions, including personalized covers, corporate imprints, and excerpts, can be created in large quantities for special needs. For more information, contact the publisher.

We are always looking for people to write books on new and related subjects. If you have an idea for a book, please contact us at proposals@schifferbooks.com.

For the many reasons to smile

For the amazing people we celebrate in this book

For Anna, who is our inspiration

For you, dear reader

Introduction

How would you feel if you looked for a book about a specific topic that didn't exist? This happened to me in 1989.

Hi, I'm Anna's Mom. My daughter is a young adult who is all that and a bag of chips—and oh, by the way, she was born with Down syndrome. When her friends see me, they say, "Hi, Anna's Mom!" My identity has become synonymous with my daughter's.

Anna was born during a rare November ice storm in the middle of the night. That morning, a nurse came into my hospital room and said, "God has a big job for you!" in a solemn tone. Later in the day, a photographer came to me and said, "I guess you don't want pictures of your baby, do you?" Another nurse said, "Are you accepting your flowers?" I felt like I was in a bad movie. Didn't these people know that I just gave birth to my beautiful third daughter? I was too happy that she was alive to be angry at their ignorance and insensitivity, and too concerned how to have the right words to express to my two older daughters anticipating the arrival of their new baby sister.

When Anna was born in 1989, I wanted to know how to talk to my daughters about their baby sister and the new experiences we will all encounter together. At that time, they were five and twelve years old. Honestly, I wanted to know the right way to talk to them in a positive way about Down syndrome. So, I asked my nurse if I could have a visit from the hospital pastor or social worker to seek counsel and advice.

A social worker visited me that day, and she said, "The way you handle the new addition to your family is the way your daughters will handle the news as well. If you're relaxed and accepting, then they will follow. If you're upset, they will be too."

I asked the social worker if she had a book or any reading material I could read about people with Down syndrome, especially of a child's development at two, five, and ten years of age and into young adulthood. I expressed I wanted to know how she would talk, play, and grow with her siblings; what the experience of puberty would be like; what school would be like; and would she be able to read, ride a bike, get married? I was lost and needed answers, stories, pictures, support—anything! She told me there was no such book or material out there.

Around the same time my daughter was born, people were starting to think differently about people with Down syndrome. (I now say "different abilities" instead of disabilities.) The new buzzwords were "reaching your true

potential." Yes, that is what I wanted. I wanted Anna to reach her true potential, be independent, enjoy her life! Wasn't there a book out there for my husband and me to navigate our new journey? Unfortunately, there wasn't. I was shocked and surprised that I needed to leave the hospital without a road map with our precious baby. At that moment, I thought that someday I would like to write the book and show the road map to help others the way I needed help and guidance.

It was on the second day that I realized my reality and others in the hospital were worlds apart with their antiquated ways of treating new parents with special babies. I was ecstatic to hold Anna in my arms and wanted to run out right away.

The social worker had great wisdom and sensed I was wrestling with a variety of emotions. She expressed that I would have a best friend my whole life, but it would not be easy, and I would find strength in the many milestones that Anna would reach. "The things that came easily to your other two daughters will be lifelong challenges with your new baby. She will need you every day of her life, but she will keep you young, as she will have the heart of a child but teach you along the way," she told me. Yes, my ideas were much different. I then knew how to join my own ideas of raising Anna and her sisters with faith and perfect love with the insight, prayers, and godly counsel I received! Meeting the social worker was a blessing. Her words have resonated with me many times through my daughter's life, especially since she was born on Thanksgiving—what a blessing!

I finally found my strength to go home and bring the family together with my three daughters and my husband through faith, comfort, encouragement, love, and support by people who knew how to come alongside a new mom—yes, Anna's Mom.

ANDREA KNAUSS
COEDITOR

About this Book

The idea to make a book with my mother began in the year 2015. I was beginning to fall more in love with publishing and the idea that communities can grow around a single book idea. I had always known my mom's desire to create helpful information for families, and I thought it would be wonderful to help her make one of her dreams come true and work together with her. Growing up, I remember her working with magazines to provide resources for families of children with special needs. I admired that about her, and the idea must have resonated with me. She also talked often about her desire to create a book just like this one you hold in your hands, for families who may benefit from real stories, from real people.

And that's what this book is. Real people with real stories. Raw, truthful, and relatable. A lot has happened since we first conceived the idea to put this book together. The emotional landscape of the world has changed dramatically. But that doesn't stop the need for stories. In fact, it increases the demand. Stories help us see ourselves in others. They help us realize we're not alone.

Shortly after the launch of the first edition of *Reasons to Smile*, I gave birth to a premature little boy. I found myself in a similar situation as my mother in 1989—searching for a book for answers. I knew nothing about prematurity, and I wanted to know what to expect. Thankfully, I found a helpful resource. But it helped me relate with this book even more so. It helped me see how important it truly is to hear from others who have been down a similar road and are at the other end extending a hand, telling you everything is going to be fine.

At this time, I sit around a table with my mother, my little sister Anna, and my son, and we make scribbles in the (what is to be) revised edition of *Reasons to Smile,* and we make room in our hearts for whom this book might reach next.

Thank you to everyone who has been a part of the *Reasons to Smile* book community. From the helpers who put the books in new baby baskets to the organizations who have listed it as an important resource, to the new parents and grandparents who keep the book on their coffee table and read a story here and there. We thank you deeply.

ELIZABETH MARTINS
COEDITOR

FOREWORD

A Note from Keith Harris

On a cold and wet January morning in 1986, I felt certain that I'd never again have a reason to smile. On January 21 of that year, the second of my four sons, Timothy, was born. A few hours after his birth, our doctor told me that our newborn son had Down syndrome. My world faded instantly to black, and I felt that all hope for the future was gone.

If I'd only known then what I know now, I would have definitely found my reasons to smile. I would have known that my son's birth would indeed change everything but that it would turn out to be the best thing that's ever happened to my family—not the worst. I find it very amusing now that I could be so, so wrong.

I'm Keith Harris, and my wife Jeannie and I have four amazing adult sons. In 2010, we helped our son Tim follow his dream to open his own business—a restaurant in Albuquerque, New Mexico, called Tim's Place. It's open seven days a week and serves breakfast, lunch, and hugs. Tim insisted that something called a "Tim Hug" be featured on his menu. It's become the most popular item on his menu, and most people order at least one. He even has an electronic hug counter on the wall. The counter is approaching 75,000 hugs. In July of 2014, Tim even got to deliver one of his famous hugs to President Barack Obama and his wife Michelle in the White House.

In the past couple of years, Tim's story has gone viral. His story has been told by major media outlets all around the world. He has millions of followers in over one hundred countries. People from more than thirty countries have made the trek to Albuquerque to meet Tim in person. It's a "bucket list" phenomenon for many people from all walks of life.

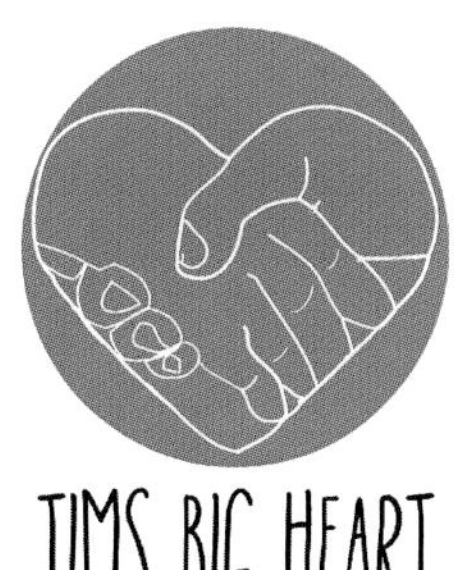

In September of 2014, our family helped Tim open part two of his dream—a 501(c)3 non-profit called Tim's Big Heart Foundation. The Foundation is dedicated to helping families around the world that have a family member with an intellectual disability and their own dream to start a small business. Tim wants others to reach their dreams too. It's his own way of paying it forward.

Since 2012 when Tim's story went viral, my wife and I have received over 7,000 personal letters from families around the world. Most of these families have a child living with Down syndrome and want to let us know how Tim's story has inspired them. It's deeply satisfying and moving for us to know that Tim's success has inspired so many others. Tim's story, however, is just one story. Over the past three decades, we've met hundreds of amazing families who have a child living with Down syndrome. Every single one of these families has inspired us and has a story that needs to be told.

Earlier this year, I had the good fortune to be contacted by Elizabeth Martins and her mom Andrea Knauss. Elizabeth shared with me her family's vision to create a book that would be a platform for families around the world to share their stories about celebrating life with a person with Down syndrome. Through lots of hard work and perseverance, Elizabeth and Andrea have collected a breathtaking portfolio of stories. Each of the stories is real, written from the heart, and is a genuine gift for you — only waiting to be opened.

As the father of a young man with Down syndrome who's working hard each and every day to make his mark on the world and whose story is inspiring others, I can tell you that this book is very, very important. It's important because we all need to share our stories to let the world know about the profound beauty that exists in the hearts and minds of families that have a child with Down syndrome. Sadly for us, we can't always share our thoughts and feelings face to face. Fortunately for us, though, sometimes a book like this one comes along and we can share our experiences in a way that matters and that provides hope, comfort, and support to us all.

My sincere hope is that this book is only the beginning of this project and that other books will soon follow. It's important to me, and it's vitally important and necessary for our world and the countless families that can be reached in this way.

Can you believe that I'm the same man that thought his world was shattered in 1986? I was wrong, and I'm so very, very happy that I was. Everything changed for me that day, and my eyes and my heart are wide open in a way that I never could have imagined.

You're in for a real treat, dear reader. Find your favorite place to sit. Still your mind from the hustle and bustle of your life and open your heart. Savor the pages to come like I have. I wish you much love and happiness. I also wish for you the purity of heart and soul that I see when I look in my son's eyes. In closing, I wish you many, many reasons to smile!

With much love, respect, and gratitude,

Keith Harris

Albuquerque, New Mexico

Stories

Adele's Story

Krista Rowland-Collins
High River, Alberta, Canada

We found out about Adele's diagnosis early on in our pregnancy. It was a difficult time for us, with emotions running on high. Our minds raced. Our doubts and fears took over. Our hopes of having a perfect child shattered right before our eyes. We thought that the perfect child would be one without Down syndrome. How could we raise a child with additional needs? Are we strong enough? Would we be good parents? Our thoughts were so clouded by statistics. It was overwhelming and our hearts ached. We were facing the unknown. Emotions had taken over logic; we needed to grieve.

Three weeks later, at our eighteen-week ultrasound, we saw this perfect little miracle, flailing her arms and legs and bouncing all around. She wasn't a baby with Down syndrome anymore. She was just our baby. We fell madly in love with this little being whom we had not even met.

Today, we have a beautiful daughter. There are no limits for Adele; there are only hopes and dreams, resilience, love, and encouragement from the world around her.

When I look into Adele's eyes, I see strength, courage, and beauty. I see right into her soul. I see a beautiful angel who has had an impact on many lives in such a short period of time. I see that she has changed so many views and perspectives, and she has done this not only in our town, but all across the world. Adele has taught me about diversity. She has taught me about patience, about slowing down and enjoying the little moments throughout the day.

I am your mommy, Adele. I will always look after you. I will always advocate for you. I will always hug you when you need a hug, although it is your hugs that bring the most comfort. I will always show others that you came into this world for a reason. You were given to us for a reason. You are a miracle, my sweet Adele.

Adele's Baskets

After hearing too many heart-wrenching stories about families being encouraged to terminate or being told "I'm sorry" after receiving a Down syndrome diagnosis, I knew it was time to start Adele's Baskets. Although Adele's diagnosis caught us by surprise, we are grateful for all that she has brought to our lives and to those around her.

Our mission is to provide families with comfort and reassurance, and most importantly, that each family hears the word "CONGRATULATIONS!" Every life has value. Every baby should be welcomed into the world with excitement and love.

To date, our team has delivered hundreds of welcome baskets to very deserving families in Calgary, Red Deer, Edmonton, Lethbridge, and other parts of Canada. The baskets are filled with beautiful gifts as well as a photo shoot and a list of resources to get the family started on their journey. We sit with families in their hospital rooms. We cry. We laugh. We understand. We get it. It's an unexpected journey, but it's one that is filled with love, light, and joy.

For more information on Adele's Baskets, visit @aperfectextrachromosome on Instagram.

While we try to teach our children all about life,
our children teach us what life is all about.

Angela Schwidt

Sibling Bond

Anila Jolly
Buckinghamshire, England

I am the younger sister, and only sibling, of a wonderful brother born with Down syndrome in the early 1960s. For my brother, positivity, joy, and happiness are routine. He has thrived, despite the difficulties of the era in which he was born, and has shown remarkable resilience through life's traumas. I love him dearly and he is the "centrepiece," the focal point, of our little family. My brother is truly the most life-affirming gift my parents gave to me and I thank them—deeply.

My brother's uplifting personality, loyalty, and perceptiveness have been a very powerful and edifying influence on my own life and character. He has taught me the meaning of unconditional love and how to care. As a young child I seemed to know his vulnerability, and my sensitivity and attentiveness towards him grew. Our bond has strengthened from my innate need to "be there" for him. Down syndrome does not define him; he is my brother, someone whom I tried to include in my childhood activities with others. He, in turn, has the skill to know exactly when I am in need of cheering and bolstering. His favourite phrase is "Don't worry, be happy!" This began when he saw me getting stressed as a teenager doing my exams. My brother is also, therefore, our in-house philosopher. And his hugs are renowned!

My devotion has deepened through the years. As an adult, I have come to realise my vocation to support him into the future. I will be his greatest guide and strongest advocate for the ongoing road. I will be there fulfilling my role, in loco parentis, when that time comes. This, I feel, is the lasting legacy that my parents will leave to my brother. I want them to know the depth of my determination to look out for him—always.

I would like parents of children with Down syndrome to know the unbreakable strength of the sibling bond, an invisible thread that connects us to our brother or sister. We love them with an unrivalled fervour, and we are as equally fierce in our allegiance to them as they are in their devotion to us. We will always need, and want, our parents to support us and love us as we take over the reins. And our love will guide us, as we usher our brother or sister through that time when "Mummy's gone to God."

For me, I know that my brother's strength will be my own personal lodestar; that he will hold on to my hand tightly, and lead me into our future—together.

A brother is a friend given by Nature.

Jean Baptiste Legouve

Sisterhood Is a Journey

Elizabeth Martins
Philadelphia, Pennsylvania

Before you were born, I wanted to meet you. I asked Mom for a baby sister, and she answered my wish by telling me, "A new baby sister is on the way. But," she said, "she's not any new baby sister. She's a special baby sister." I couldn't wait to kiss you and hold you, special or not.

We used to take bubble baths together, baby sister. When I threw the squeaky bath toys in the air, we watched as they cascaded into the water and splashed us in our faces. It was silly, but it made you crack up. I can still remember your tummy-tingling laughter. Sometimes, you were upset if too much water splashed your eyes, but we always had a cloth nearby.

Baby sister, when we would walk around the neighborhood together, I held your hand tightly. I didn't want anyone to hurt you. You were MY baby sister, and no one would place a pinky on you or say anything that would make you sad. I made sure of it.

Baby sister, when we were both teens on a camping trip, you fell from the red kayak. I think the boys were rocking it. Into the creek you plunged, but your orange vest kept you afloat. You laughed it off, but I think you were a bit cautious of kayaks after that.

Baby sister, when I started going to friend's houses without you, it wasn't easy. I thought of you at home, unable to be with me all the time. I thought I wasn't allowed to have fun if you weren't having fun. No one knew I felt this way—not Mom, not Dad, not you, and even I had trouble placing this feeling.

Baby sister, when I moved away from home and started my own family, I thought of you every night before sleep and wished there was something I could do to save you. It took me a while to realize you didn't need to be saved. You would visit me on weekends, and I would take you to restaurants and show you the time of your life! But I would soon come to learn that we had the most fun just staying inside my apartment, being silly.

Baby sister, you are a grown woman now. A wonderful aunt. Sometimes, I catch myself telling you what to do, but then I remember to stop. You are confident and speak what's on your mind; you tell me when you prefer things to be quiet and when you're ready for fun. I don't run around trying to prove anything to anyone anymore. We simply are together. It is quieter; it is peaceful. We are growing more into womanhood together; we are facing the unknown. When we're together, I whisper that I'll always be there for you, and I mean it. When you look at me and smile, you tell me the same. In our quiet new world together, I finally realize that sisterhood is not a destination. It is a journey.

You may be as different as the sun and the moon, but the same blood flows through both your hearts. You need her, as she needs you.

George R.R. Martin

Finding Joy

Alyssa & Ashley Ng
Singapore

At seven months old, Andrea was diagnosed with type 1 diabetes, making her dependent on insulin injections thrice a day. Through the years, she mastered controlling her sugar intake and independently administering the right dosage of insulin. Growing up, while parents moderated their children's sweets to prevent a sugar high, Andrea possessed an ironclad discipline to consume only as much as she knew she could, turning down excess food that would affect her diabetes.

Being born the third child in a family of five daughters, this inevitably spurs a competitive spirit and drive to outshine her siblings. No dream is too big for our sister, and she attacks life with exuberance and confidence that never fails to inspire us. When she decided to join her school's swim team, her diligence and discipline allowed her to excel in the sport, clinching numerous trophies in the national championships organized by the Singapore Sports Council for the Disabled.

The most admirable thing about Andrea is her fearless attitude and courage in trying her hand at everything. Besides joining her school's sailing team, bowling team, and Chinese orchestra, Andrea would sign herself up for anything that caught her interest, without a second thought! (Even community cooking classes!) We constantly take strength from her courage in boldly trying new things and starting humbly from scratch.

Once Andrea completed her formal schooling, she decided to start volunteering in our parish. Four times a week, she would independently travel there to help out for the day; a testament to the selfless and generous spirit that Andrea possesses. A few months later, she decided that she wanted to get a job, since she wanted to "support the family." During her arduous job-hunting process, she would pass by shops advertising vacancies and inquire on her suitability, excited and hopeful with its "No Experience Needed" requirement. Despite countless rejections, her unwavering optimism fueled her with the same enthusiasm and eagerness as if starting on a clean slate each time.

In time, she found what she terms her "dream job" as a part-time waitress at Crossings Café in Singapore, since she gets to meet new people every day. Sometimes, she even pleads with our parents to allow her to work on weekends. Andrea is blessed with the special gift of finding joy in every little thing, and it continues to bring her endless delight each time a customer gives her a tip (not customary in our local culture).

Just like every parent can relate to, it is difficult to articulate the light and spirit that each individual child brings into a family. However, we can say with utmost confidence that God did right by this world in gifting Andrea to us. Thus, in response to why God made Andrea the way He did, it's for Andrea to keep shining the way she does. The world definitely needs more of her light.

With tremendous burdens often come enormous gifts.
The trick is to identify the gifts, and glory in them.

Dr. Maya Shetreat-Klein

Dream Big

Dylan Kuehl
Olympia, Washington

I was featured in the original *Reasons to Smile* book, but when I was featured, it was my mom who shared my goals, dreams, and accomplishments. Five years later, I'm proud to be writing my own story to share with you all. When the first feature was written, I had a goal to attend my local college. Now, I'm a senior at the Evergreen State College, and my academic dreams are coming true. I'm the first person with Down syndrome to attend a four-year university in Washington State, in the United States of America.

A lot led into getting to this point. To do the work, I needed my "YES team"; family, professors, mentors, and peers who were willing to support me on my journey. If you want to go to school, you need to ask for help, and it takes a village to get a degree.

The most important key to my schooling is that it's okay to struggle and fail; in the end, you will succeed. There were times where it was really tough, but I kept going and I didn't give up. If you believe it, there's nothing that can stop you. Just put your mind to it and get it done.

One of my first goals started in 2005—an art business called DK Arts. With DK Arts, I go to conferences and art festivals to sell my art. It's still strong today. DK Arts started because I needed a job where I could be interactive with my community. Other jobs didn't fit my needs, so I created a business that would. I created something to showcase my abilities.

I have many dreams for the future. Once I graduate college in spring of 2022, I would like to develop my very own video game. I also want to write a musical and perform in it. Of course, I want to jam with my band, the Inclusionaires, and keep on playing music.

That's how I've gotten this far. I'm a dancer, a bowler, a musician, a scholar, an artist, and an advocate. Most importantly though, I'm a dreamer. My message is simple: it's about abilities, not disabilities. This powerful message inspires me and others to reach their dreams. Throughout my life, I have done so many things. From founding an art business to attending college and forming a band, I dream BIG. I don't let my disability get in the way of what I love to do. Instead, I let my abilities shine. Never let anyone tell you that you can't do it, because if I can, you can too.

Keep on living the dream!

For more information on DK Arts, visit www.oly-wa.us/dkarts.

I choose not to place "DIS" in my ability.

Robert M. Hensel

Jenna

Joanne Reece, Jacqueline Guishard, & Evette Reece
Mississauga, Ontario, Canada

Jenna is our angel, a special gift from God who has brought joy, love, and laughter into our family's lives. Jenna loves giving and receiving hugs; she will tell you they make her feel better. She has taught us the importance of speaking your truth by being yourself no matter what. Jenna shines her light in this world through her love of birthdays, hugs, laughter, dance, drama, and music.

Jenna has made changes in the school system through her ability to express her truth. Her school years have seen her shuffled between programs instead of the staff understanding her learning style and needs. Jenna senses people and needs time to get to know someone; when she was finally placed in a school that understood this, Jenna blossomed and was awarded the Yes I Can Award for the Arts.

Jenna has many strengths and one of her natural gifts is her dramatic talent. She has a love for the stage and her audiences adore her humour and ability to bring to life the many characters she has played. As a child Jenna watched the movie *Annie* daily, and she knew the lines of the different characters. Her spotlight moment came when she portrayed the role of Ms. Hannigan. She had the audience captivated with pure delight, with her arms and hips swaying and her perfect high-pitched tone. A true Oscar moment. Jenna is a part of Drama-way, a theatre group that focuses on students' capabilities.

Jenna, being the radiant star that she is, has a passion for movies; the Disney movies make up her special collection. Jenna will watch her favourite movies for hours. Her movies bring together her love of music and theatre, as she sings aloud while watching *Frozen, Brave*, and *The Princess and the Frog*, to name a few!

Another one of Jenna's strengths that gives her family many reasons to smile is her sense of humour and her ability to make others laugh. There was a time when Jenna became silent due to the transition from childhood to adolescence, and we saw her bright light become dim. However, Jenna bounced back, shining brighter than ever, and she constantly amazes us with her quick-witted sense of humour. We often say, "Jenna is a hoot! She is so hilarious!" especially when people ask how she is.

Jenna is passionate about birthdays and birthdays are a big deal in our family. Jenna has embraced this wholeheartedly. At her Sweet Sixteen she walked the red carpet to greet her guests and any paparazzi that may have crashed the affair. Upon meeting a total stranger, she will ask their name and then inquire when their birthday is. She can tell you the birth dates of everyone within her inner circle, including her favorite teachers. So, Jenna wants to know: When is your birthday?

What lies behind us and what lies before us
are tiny matters compared to what lies within us.

Ralph Waldo Emerson

No Limits

Amy Cajigas
Shamong, New Jersey

A little person came into my life and surpassed all expectations that the diagnosis of Down syndrome said he would. A child that brought more joy into my life by making me a Mama for the seventh time. When people told us that we should be done and that we had enough, something was calling my soul, something inside that told me that there was supposed to be one more child . . . it was him all along telling me that he needed to be here, he had a job to do, and I was to be a part of it—his Mama.

Emanual was born on February 17, 2011, and although he was born six weeks early, he was a fighter, proving people wrong by becoming a super breastfeeding baby who, for two years, nursed like a champ! He endured open-heart surgery at fifteen months old and was home in three days. He continued to break the stereotypes of a baby with Down syndrome by walking at eighteen months and reaching all his physical therapy goals by two and a half years old. By this time, Manny was involved in the Young Athletes program for Special Olympics and again was amazing everyone with his athletic abilities. Manny could shoot basketballs into the hoops (some of them three-pointers) with a persistence of someone far older than he was. He could dribble a soccer ball across the field, never using his hands, and scoring right in the goal with a powerful and accurate kick.

When Manny was at his first Olympic summer games at two and a half, he raced in the future-stars race, and a local photographer snapped a picture of him. The Young Athletes program asked us if they could use the photo for their Wawa fundraising campaign! Manny's picture was all over New Jersey in Wawas and stores promoting the Young Athletes program!

He is now three years old (at the time of this writing) and continues to amaze us every day. He is the only three-year-old in the strider bike program at Special Olympics learning to ride a balance bike! He is starting a regular three-year-old preschool program in the fall. He is testing age appropriate or above average in all areas except for his expressive language! That is the only therapy he receives once a week, and he is saying more and more words every day! This child has so much love and support from his six siblings. He is going to move mountains, break stereotypes, and reach his dreams. His picture has inspired so many children just like him to never set limits and to expect the best no matter what!

So glad to be his Mama. No limits, Manny.

I love you.

Limitations only go so far.

Robert M. Hensel

Welcome to Holland

Emily Perl Kingsley
Briarcliff Manor, New York

When you're going to have a baby, it's like planning a fabulous vacation trip to Italy. You buy several guide books and make all your wonderful plans. The Coliseum. The Michelangelo David. The Gondolas in Venice. You may learn some handy phrases in Italian. It's all a very exciting time. After months of eager anticipation, the day finally arrives. You pack your bags and off you go. Several hours later, the plane lands and the pilot announces, "Welcome to Holland."

"Holland?" you say. "What do you mean Holland? We signed up for Italy. We are supposed to be in Italy. All our lives we've dreamed of going to Italy."

There was a change in the flight plan. You've landed in Holland and there you must stay.

The very important thing to remember is that you haven't landed in a bad place, it's just a different place. There has been a change in plans for you.

So you must go out and buy new guide books. And you must learn a new language. And you will meet a whole new group of people you would not have met in Italy.

Holland is slower-paced than Italy, less flashy. But after you've been there for a while and you catch your breath and you look around, you begin to notice that Holland has windmills . . . and Holland has tulips. Holland has Rembrandts.

A lot of people you know are busy coming and going from Italy . . . and they're all talking about what a wonderful time they had. And for a while, from time to time, you may say, "Yes, that's where we were supposed to go. That's what we had planned." The loss of that dream can be a signif-icant loss.

But, if you spend too much time mourning the fact that you didn't get to Italy, you may never be free to enjoy the very special, the very lovely, the very beautiful and perfect things . . . about Holland.

We must let go of the life we have planned,
so as to accept the one that is waiting for us.

Joseph Campbell

Every Step

Jenn Ng Miu Leng
Singapore

We first shared a story with the editors of *Reasons to Smile* when Marcus was just a baby. Now he is seven. Since then, we have gone through many doctor appointments and therapies and have learned so much. As the years went by, the initial fears were replaced by happy memories, from him speaking his first words to him writing his first sentence. Picking up new skills such as changing his own clothes, showering himself, and finally moving to his own bed. He is my little big boy.

Thanks to the many people who gave him a chance, he learned to ride a bicycle and picked up drumming and swimming. In his free time, he loves to sing and dance. His current favorite song is "Butter" by BTS (Korean pop group). He enjoys reading Dr. Seuss's Big Books of Beginner Books and the *Kids Bible* nightly. This brave little one has also tried climbing up a tight ladder to swing on a trapeze, ride on an all-terrain vehicle (ATV), and even zip-lining across a forest in Phuket.

However, one of the most important milestones would be him getting baptized last Christmas. Seeing how he is able to attend mass, sing the songs in church, and bow with reverence whenever he goes up to receive the blessing brings joy to my heart. Never one to forget about grace before meals, he is also the one that reminds the whole family to thank God. Every week, in my prayers, I am reminded again how truly blessed I am to have him as my son.

Ever caring, he will be the first person to come and ask how I am feeling when I am down, and his hug would melt away all my worries and pain. He has taught me to appreciate all the little things in life.

I can't imagine what life would be like without him.

Children remind us to treasure the smallest
of gifts, even in the most difficult times.

Allen Klein

Superheroes

Jenny Asbury
Harlington, Bedfordshire, England

Last year was very challenging for our family as my dad became very ill. He was living independently on his own nearby but was diagnosed with terminal pancreatic cancer.

Our family spent our time caring for him around the clock. Michael, my son with Down syndrome, loved visiting Grandad Magic. Michael was eight years old. Grandad would teach him to play draughts and there was always a KitKat for him in the fridge for them to share.

They spent many happy times together chatting and sharing magic tricks.

As time went on my dad became weaker and confined to his bed. Michael still enjoyed visiting him, but we limited this in his final stages, as we didn't want him to be remembered like this.

One afternoon, we came home after what we had decided would be one of Michael's final visits. Michael sat at our kitchen table and was busy drawing a picture. No one took much notice of him as we were all so wrapped up in our own grief.

Later, I approached Michael. His picture was the most detailed I'd ever seen him do, with many different coloured smiling faces and a big yellow sun in the corner. I praised him for such a great picture and asked him to explain to me what it was.

Pointing to the sun: "This is the sun, Mummy, it's going to help grandad get better."

Pointing to the faces: "These are all my superheroes, they are going to fly grandad to heaven for me."

I was so proud of him and took it straight over to my dad's house and pinned it next to his bed. He was now in a coma state, but I believe he was able to hear me so I described the picture and explained Michael's wish for him. He gently squeezed my hand with all his strength.

Meanwhile, I scoured the Internet for bereavement books for children with special needs. Michael had never experienced death of a close relative; how could I really prepare him for this?

Grandad Magic passed away a week later at home with his family by his side. Michael's brother and sister were caring for Michael at home. I returned home with a stone in my heart knowing I had to break the news to our children. I took Christopher (16) and Sarah (14) aside and gave them the sad news that they knew was inevitable.

Michael was happily playing his music so I went up to him, sat next to him on the sofa, and told him that Grandad Magic had gone to heaven.

Michael looked at me for a moment then punched his fist in the air and with the broadest grin said, "Yes, they did it!"

Ever since my dad's death, Michael often has his invisible superheroes by his side when playing on his own. They are there to comfort him and I've no doubt his grandad is one of them.

The best and most beautiful things in the world cannot be seen or even touched—they must be felt with the heart.

Helen Keller

Blessing

Joan Kozak
Whittier, California

Twenty-five years ago, I thought my world had ended. What started as the most exciting day in my life, ended up as the worst. My first child was born, and thirty minutes after delivery, the doctors told us he had Down syndrome. I couldn't listen to what the doctors were saying. I had never met anyone with Down syndrome.

Meanwhile, while I was feeling sorry for myself, my son Jared was fighting for his life. He had aspirated meconium, which is similar to a tar substance; it had gone into his lungs. He was in intensive care and couldn't breathe on his own. My husband went to see him and came back very excited, so proud of his son. I couldn't understand how my husband could be so proud of this child with Down syndrome. I felt miserable that I couldn't give him a "normal" son.

Later that evening, they brought Jared into my room in an incubator. A doctor was using a pump, breathing manually for him, and he was hooked up to so many tubes. They said they had to transport him right away to another department for an experimental procedure. I watched them wheel him away still having never touched, let alone held, him.

All of a sudden, something kicked in. That was my son they were taking away. I knew I had to be with him. At that moment, the Down syndrome didn't matter. I just wanted my son to survive. We checked out early and went to the hospital.

The doctor explained the procedure. He would be put on an iron lung. A tube would be attached to his carotid artery, in his neck. This would allow the blood to come out, be cleansed in the iron lung, and put back into his body. They could only leave it in for ten days. After the doctor explained everything, he said, "You don't have to agree to the surgery. Jared has a hole in his heart, he had several seizures, his lungs won't be strong, will always get pneumonia, and he may never walk or talk!" I asked what would happen if we decided not to do the surgery. He said, "He will die." My husband and I didn't even need to discuss it; we both said, "Do the surgery!"

They hooked Jared up that day. After only three days they were able to take him off. He was breathing on his own!

Jared has been a blessing in our lives. I can't imagine my life without him! I would love to take him back to the doctor who told us he may never walk or talk! Jared is an actor (two films and a web series), works at a restaurant, attends college, ushers at our local theater house, and plays Special Olympic basketball, soccer, and bowling. Seizure free, and he's never had pneumonia!

The human spirit is stronger than
anything that can happen to it.

C. C. Scott

Left-Handed

Fionn Crombie Angus
County Clare, Ireland

For years, I've had three main interests: wildlife of the world, photography and video making, and Irish traditional music. Now that I've graduated high school, I'm exploring these full time, with my dad at my side.

We put together presentations about animals that we bring to local school children, and the Heritage Council has awarded me Heritage Expert status. I'm the youngest person in Ireland to receive this award. Sometimes when I give talks I stutter a bit. But people are really patient, and I just work it through. My dad says that students learn as much from who I am as from what I talk about.

We've started a project making videos, called Fionnathan Productions (my name is Fionn and my dad's name is Jonathan). Our first film was for charity, showing people with Down syndrome just living normal, wonderful lives. Since then, I have interviewed film makers and movie stars, musicians and politicians, restaurateurs and zookeepers, scientists and scholars, authors and athletes; some with disabilities, all interesting. The question I ask most is "What do you love about your life?" because it encourages people to speak from the heart.

We've been featured in newspapers, radio, and TV. When a talk show host asked me how it feels to have Down syndrome, I asked him how it feels to not have Down syndrome. That got a big laugh from the studio audience—and from the folks at home, probably. One film I made was shortlisted for the Young Film Maker of the Year Award (but I didn't win). I may decide that this is the work I want to do in the future, but there's plenty of time to figure that out. I'll probably go to college first.

I've played the violin for most of my life. I like pop music and classical, but traditional Irish music is my favourite. Sometimes I join a session in the local pub, but they play so fast it's hard to keep up. Busking is a great way to meet people and put a skip in their step. I've played all around Ireland. I love to share my music, and people are often surprised to see me. Recently a woman came up and said, "I'm impressed that you play so well, given the fact that you are left-handed." But that's just one of the things that makes me unique.

For more information on Fionnathan Productions, visit www.facebook.com/Fionnathan and www.bit.ly/WhatDoYouLoveAboutYourLife.

Go as far as you can see; when you get there,
you'll be able to see further.

Thomas Carlyle

Love of Life

Karen Gregoire
Chicopee, Massachusetts

Sometimes a person comes into your life and changes everything! For our Josh, who was born with an incredible LOVE for LIFE, that person came from an unexpected place. A place we never would have dreamed up in a million years.

A few years ago, Josh signed up for a martial arts class through a local agency. On his third class, instructor Ken asked Josh, "Would you like to break something?" And just like magic, a new path was forged. Josh has gained an incredible amount of confidence through his martial arts training, now ranked a green belt, and has gained an entire "breaking family" through his participation in the United States and World Breaking Association (USBA/WBA).

Josh competed in his first board-breaking tournament in November 2018, as a white belt, winning FIRST place against neurotypical martial artists both in power wood hand and his creative breaking routine. There was not a dry eye in the house.

Josh has competed in too-many-to-count-or-remember breaking tournaments, earning many awards but, more importantly, earning much respect from the martial arts community.

Everything Josh has learned from his martial arts training and competitive breaking tournaments has carried forward into the rest of his life. He is capable of so many things we never thought possible, never gave much thought to, or just simply didn't expect he could accomplish. He is more serious. More focused. He has been working a steady part-time job for more than two years, earning competitive wages. He takes care of his apartment and his own schedule without much help from family.

I believe that Josh's progress and explosion toward independence was the direct result of the first non-family member becoming very involved in his life. Instructor Ken not only has continued to be his instructor, coach, and mentor but has become a father figure, big brother, boss, personal trainer, and best friend. At this point in their journey, I often wonder who needs each other more, Josh needing Ken or Ken needing Josh. What I know for sure is that Josh continues his LOVE of LIFE.

Josh's journey can be followed at www.bit.ly/JustJoshinYa.

The only disability in life is a bad attitude.

Scott Hamilton

A Love Story

Maria Elena Walters
Miami, Florida

My only child, my daughter Monica, was born ten days before my twentieth birthday.

I was young and healthy, and had a perfectly normal pregnancy. Monica was born with Down syndrome, which at that time was thought to only occur when the mother was over forty.

When the pediatrician delivered the news to me, he stood at the foot of my bed and said, "Your daughter is a mongoloid," turned and left, offering no words of encouragement or referrals to support groups or educators.

On the day of my twentieth birthday, I took my baby to our local university's medical school child development center, and the director informed me that my daughter would never walk or talk and that, given my youth, I should institutionalize her. I was stunned by both of these people's ignorance and insensitivity.

I was very scared, and without access to any information or support groups, as these were nonexistent in 1972, I had no idea where to begin helping her. But fortunately, Monica and I were not alone: my parents were there every step of the way, giving us unconditional love and endless support, and my child thrived!

Monica's life has been wonderful, in spite of all the naysayers. The most basic human need is love; everyone wants someone of their own, but not everyone is lucky enough to find that person. Monica did! She met her husband David at school, when she was nineteen and he thirteen. A few years passed and the age difference became less noticeable. In the summer of 2000, they began dating, and on Christmas Day 2001, they became engaged. In March 2005 they were married in a lovely and memorable ceremony. My niece made a documentary about their relationship, called *Monica and David*, to show people that we can all aspire to, and find, love, in spite of those who would try to tell us otherwise.

Monica and David volunteer at a school for children and young adults with intellectual challenges, and participate in several sports competitions through Special Olympics.

They recently celebrated their tenth anniversary, and are very happy, never arguing or disagreeing. They live for each other and are a wonderful example of how all married couples should treat one another.

In the end, Monica walked, danced, talked, learned two languages, and got married! Don't let anyone tell you there is no hope; my daughter and her husband are living proof that hope never dies and that people with Down syndrome can lead active, productive, happy lives! Those who are fortunate enough to be a parent, sibling, or friend to a person with Down syndrome will quickly learn how deep and unconditional love is, and that it is forever!

For more about the documentary on Monica and David, visit www.monicaanddavid.com.

Spread love everywhere you go. Let no one ever come to you without leaving happier.

Mother Teresa

This Is Happiness

Liza Øverdal
Ålgård, Norway

I am often asked by others to describe my daughter, people are naturally curious about the unknown. I find this difficult as she is what is "normal" for me, and in the busy day-to-day schedule, I tend to focus on the now and not what makes her or my family different. But, luckily she reminds me of what makes her unique, often when I need it the most.

Selina wears her soul on the outside, like an extra layer of skin; it is open for all to see and feel. Her presence is felt in every room of the house. Her enthusiasm over everyday joys can be heard on the mountaintops; she shares them with everyone she meets on her path. Her love of everything, from puppies to small rocks, which fit in her jacket pocket—I am envious of its pureness.

She experiences all of life's ups and downs with her soul exposed, and includes us all in it. We feel her joy, we feel her passion, and we feel her sorrow when things don't go as she expected. She sees no boundaries, she sees no differences—all who meet her are treated with the same interest and profound affection. There is no race, color, religion, or bias in her world.

Her rawness, her exposure, it makes us all vulnerable. As a mother I want to protect her from everything, yet she makes it clear that this is not what she wants. I worry; my view of the world is colored by assumptions and experiences—which feed my worries. Selina, however, expects more of me. She demands that we join her in her worldview, where things are simpler. Where all people are good, where everyone has good intentions, and where paying it forward is the main currency. And she reminds us every day, that this is life. This is life in its purest form, and that is certainly a reason to smile.

Knowledge of what is possible
is the beginning of happiness.

George Santayana

Hope and Joy

Gün Bilgin
Istanbul, Turkey

Thinking how to write a piece about my older son Robert Cem for this book, I began to question. How can I describe him? How can I describe his journey in life? The way he chooses to live it?

Words started forming in my head: Worthiness. Fulfillment. Vulnerability. Softness. Love. Acceptance. Perseverance. Success. Courage. Fun. Compassion . . .

Then it got me thinking further. What does fulfillment mean? How do you live a meaningful life? How do you feel worthy? Loved? Successful? Accepted? What is the single most important ingredient for him that helps him to feel all these things? How did he cope with all the inclusion struggles, the loneliness he felt at these times, the loss of loved ones, or the feeling of failure he felt at times?

I realised that there is a single, basic quality fundamental in this process; loving and accepting who you are.

Looking at his life, I see a young man who is a high school graduate with the title of class president, a full-time office employee in a big hotel, who is a successful photographer and has held three—including one international—photography exhibitions; who has been a role model and hope to tens of thousands of families with Down syndrome in Turkey.

I see a young man who fell in love with a lovely girl and courageously opened his heart to her; who still kisses his mother in public; who is so adept in technology that he teaches his grandmother how to use smart phones; who enjoys rock and folk music equally, who is a compassionate big brother and who has such a zest for life you can only join and celebrate his joy with him.

But above all, I see a young man who loves and accepts himself, comfortable in his life journey, acknowledging his challenges and rising above these, nevertheless; who is fun and joyful and compassionate and strong.

May you have a clear path ahead of you my dear Robert Cem. With life partners and friends who love and support you, appreciate you, help you learn but know when to let you grow in your own lessons, whom you teach and from whom you learn, who share their lives with you generously; a path filled with hope and joy.

I get by with a little help from my friends.

The Beatles

A Gift

Emma Taylor
Alcester, Warwickshire, England

I would like to introduce Mathew, my incredible big brother. Mathew has Down syndrome, but that's not his story . . . that's just the beginning!

Mathew was born in January 1983 and like most parents of children who have Down syndrome, ours were told of the difficulties and limitations Mathew would have to face. I am here to tell you he proved everyone wrong.

Mathew is my only brother, in between two older sisters and two younger ones.

Growing up, Mathew was a member of the local scouts group, often going camping and joining in with every activity. He loved to ride his bike, and enjoyed exploring the countryside and the local area whenever we were on holiday. Mathew attended both a school for children with special needs as well as a mainstream primary school.

At the age of seventeen, Mathew started a work experience placement from college as a gardener at Ragley Hall, a stately home close to where we live. At the end of his college course, the head gardener offered Mathew a paid job in the gardens three days a week. This made Mathew so proud, and his whole family was bursting with pride.

Mathew has a zest for life only a few people come close to. His love for his friends and family is unlimited and he is always the first to suggest a family gathering. Mathew even became the Christmas Party organiser for the gardeners where he worked.

His sense of humour often had his mesmerised audience in stitches, whether it be in the pub, at the drama group he is a part of, or watching his favourite football team play. His memory should never be questioned and he often reminds you of embarrassing situations and funny stories.

I am forever in awe of Mathew's kind spirit and gentleness, with him never having a bad word to say about anyone. He always looks for the good in people.

It was often assumed that, as Mathew's little sister, I was more of a big sister, but that couldn't be further from the truth. Just like any big brother and little sister we argued and teased one another, but he is my best friend and protector whenever I need him.

In April 2014, Mathew lost his fight with cancer, but this story I am telling you is not a sad one—it's inspirational. Despite what Mathew was going through his priority was to keep us, his family and friends, smiling.

Mathew's Down syndrome was a gift; it's what makes him incredible and he has made us the family we are.

Even now, Mathew gives me more than a million reasons to smile. He taught everyone who met him that no matter what, you can do anything. And he did, with the most beautiful smile!

Some people come into our lives, leave footprints
on our hearts, and we are never the same.

Franz Peter Schubert

Ally's Army

Margaret Stahelek
West Chester, Pennsylvania

Ally continues to amaze us. She has come so very far in her almost twelve years of life. She got her trach removed after six years and three months! She still has her feeding tube, but with the help of a feeding clinic, she is eating pureed foods by mouth. She is still nonverbal, and in addition to having Down syndrome, she was diagnosed with autism a few years ago. Her repetitive behavior was the clue, but she is one of the most social kids I know!

Ally uses an iPad and sign language to communicate. We continue to work with speech therapy in the hope that she will talk one day. She still has a leaking mitral valve and faces a fourth heart surgery, but through it all, she thrives. She has made her communion and left the church in tears of happiness. She participates in special-needs soccer and on a Challenger baseball team. She also enjoys a special-needs Girl Scout troop. Ally has always loved swimming, even with a trach, and we finally had time to get her taking swim lessons. One of her other favorite activities she just loves is carnival rides—the faster the better!

We could not have come this far without Ally's Army. This team name started through our Buddy Walk fundraiser team name, but the name is really more than that. We have Ally's core team—our family and nurses who enjoy and work with her daily. Then we have our medical team—doctors and hospital staff that we also see on a regular basis. We also have her school team, which includes teachers, friends, physical therapists, speech therapists, and occupational therapists. We have her outside-of-school team, which includes ABA therapy, feeding clinic, speech therapy, and the iPad clinic. And we have her fun team—baseball, soccer, Girl Scouts, and swimming. And last, but certainly not least, the spiritual team—her church family.

We are thankful and grateful for each and every person in Ally's Army.

The task ahead of us is never
as great as the power behind us.

Ralph Waldo Emerson

Oh, Anna

Michael Knauss
Holland, Pennsylvania

I used to be a rock star. When my wife and I started a family, I tried to continue on my musical path. But duties and priorities quickly changed. When I wasn't changing diapers, I was hustling to make a buck on night shift, juggling jobs to make ends meet. While I loved growing a family, I admittedly never took much time to slow down to appreciate the small gifts of life. Now I am a grandfather. My two older daughters have flown the coop. But my youngest daughter, Anna, who happens to have Down syndrome, remains at home. And she is my best friend.

Anna enjoys yoga, dancing, and swimming. So much swimming! The pool is her happy place. In my younger days (before kids), I never would have imagined such a life. My old life was filled with guitar riffs, gigs, partying, and dreams of a record deal. My days now are spent quietly with Anna, wondering what she wants to eat, what new movies are out, what I can teach her that will have a lasting effect, what special things will make her smile today, how I can help her enjoy her life.

When I look back on my past life, although it appeared fun and exciting from the outside, I realized I didn't have the gifts I have now. I see the world differently because of Anna, and probably because of her having Down syndrome and the extra-special different abilities she's been gifted with. I've learned the beauty of compassion, the power of listening, and the feeling of warmth when I hear my daughter's laughter. She has unconditional acceptance and love for everyone. I believe that some wait a lifetime for these gifts, and some never experience them at all. I've also realized what it means to appreciate the small things in life, and how special milestones can be in the life of someone you constantly root for, admire, and treasure.

Not too long ago, I pulled the guitar out of the closet. It had been decades since I wrote a song. But when my fingers touched the frets again, the melody came right out. And the lyrics flowed from my mouth with ease. Before I knew it, I was writing a full-fledged song. It was easy. I had passion in my heart. Anna has passed on to me her love, unfiltered confidence, and courage. The song was about her. In fact, I simply called it "Oh, Anna."

Now, Anna and I sing her special song together frequently. It's beyond amazing to see her green eyes shining back at me as I pour my love into the song for her. I remember her as a baby when I sing. How afraid I was. How nervous. What had I done wrong? But when I sing to her, when she sings back, I see the wonder of life reflected in those green eyes. And I wouldn't trade that for anything. It's not every day that you get to live and sing with an angel. I just pray that I am able to inspire her the same way she inspires me.

I used to be a rock star. I used to be alone. Now I am Anna's Dad. Together, we're both rock stars. And together, we can take on the world. She is my gift. She is my world. She is my best friend on our journey together.

Use your voice for kindness, your ears for compassion, your hands for charity, your mind for truth, and your heart for love.

Anonymous

A Great Adventure

Roz Hull
Berkeley, Gloucestershire, England

When our fourth son, Nate, was diagnosed postnatally with Down syndrome I felt like a huge rock had been dropped on me. It smashed everything I thought my future would be. In the days that followed I worried and I cried. I could physically feel the panic rising, like a huge mass of future worries; a list of insurmountable problems that awaited me. At the very top of that list was how it would affect our three older sons.

To be honest I needn't have worried. In fact, the day Nate was born, it opened up a whole new future for my boys. A future that will teach them to care and accept, to stand up for themselves and others, to be aware that "different" is okay, and to persevere even when things don't come easily.

Nate was incredibly ill for the first eight months of his life, staying mostly in hospital with tubes and machines keeping him alive. My sadness morphed into anger. I was angry that Nate was so ill and I was angry that my boys were thrown into hospital life—sick children, sad adults. Unfamiliar and scary situations were frequent; the worst of all being when they were dragged out of bed and bundled into a car early on Christmas morning because Nate had had a cardiac arrest. However, in these situations all our boys showed courage. They met very ill children, they spoke sensibly to doctors and nurses, and the beginnings of their protective love towards Nate developed. They made us proud and kept us going in extremely testing times.

Nate is now three years old and we are only at the beginning of our journey all together. He amazes us every day with his strength and determination. He makes us laugh with his cheeky smile and his innate understanding of how to entertain. The smallest success begins a Mexican wave of pride in our house. News quickly spreads from room to room of his "firsts"—his first clap, his first sign, his first step—until we are all gathered together as a captive audience, all willing him to do it again.

Don't get me wrong, it's not all sweetness and love in our house! Looking after Nate takes up a lot of my time and sometimes that causes mutters and moans. Nate can drive them mad—he breaks their Legos, rips their pictures, and (worst of all) he gets in the way of the TV! But I find this reassuringly normal; he is their younger brother and it's his job to annoy!

Today, I do not have that fear or anger that I did. Maybe I have uncertainty and I definitely have challenges—but doesn't everyone with children have those? The fact that one of our boys has Down syndrome is not our defining feature; hopefully it is that we are a happy, caring, and supportive family. I wouldn't change one thing about my journey so far, even the extremely difficult parts. It has made us who we are. Now I look forward to the future with excitement—the six of us are off on a great adventure!

Sometimes on the way to your dream,
you get lost and you find a better one.

Lisa Hammond

Winner

Sara Porter
Derby, England

Kara is a happy seven-year-old who dances, swims, and plays, and who falls in and out with her ten-year-old sister, Eloise. Like all siblings, there is the tension between who gets the best position on the sofa, who gets to listen to the car radio, and who gets my time. It's split fifty-fifty, but according to them, it's more like ninety-ten depending in favor of the other sibling! And their favorite phrase is "It's not fair!"

One of our favorite pastimes is walking through the local countryside. Kara loves car journeys, which Eloise enjoys if she has her phone or a book. Lockdown made walking part of our daily routine, and we still enjoy it.

On one drive to the countryside, Kara got very upset. She kept saying "winner" and pointing to my bag. She was getting quite annoyed that we could not understand the word she was trying to convey. We spent an hour trying to decipher what "winner" meant. Was it "dinner"? We used sign language, but still no luck. No, it was not dinner. But it was food related, we were certain.

After a bit of clever thinking, we realized she was communicating the word "window." You see, on our walks, we would journey past a coffee shop. Since it was lockdown, we could order only takeout food. We would get food from the window! Kara knew all along. So now, "winner" is our new word for our local coffee shop. Kara will always get her message across.

Later, we were at home, and I was tired. It was almost dinnertime. As a bit of a nudge, Kara went into the kitchen and placed a frying pan on my lap. Like I said, she will always get her message across! Kara loves to cook too. Once, she brought me my own cup of coffee—an entire mug of raw coffee beans. Let me tell you—the days are not boring.

Nothing in life is to be feared; it is only to be understood. Now is the time to understand more, so that we may fear less.

Marie Curie

A Letter to Myself

Sarah Roberts
Surrey, England

Two years have passed and here's the thing: life didn't go the way you planned it to, but actually it's even better than you ever could have imagined. You know those friends you thought you'd lose because your son had Down syndrome? Well you haven't. Old friendships are stronger than ever. New friendships have been formed. Friends have been your constants and you will be forever grateful. No one turned their back. You were being ridiculous.

Oh, you get to go on holiday. It's not always as relaxing as they once were . . . But you do go.

The grief you felt for the child you thought you'd lost, has long gone. It's been replaced with love, in a bucket load. Unconditional love, stronger than you ever could have hoped for.

Your family? They're just the best. Loving Oscar more deeply than you thought possible. And you know you always thought you were weak? Well, you're not anymore. You're much stronger. You hardly ever cry at rom coms like you used to.

The worrying? That hasn't stopped. You've always been a worrier, but now you focus on the here and now and enjoy it, rather than panicking about the future.

You're probably a bit nicer that you used to be. Before, you were kinda a little self-involved. Now you're mindful that other people may be going through stuff that you know nothing about. You always try to be kind.

Oh and that ludicrous notion that Chris would leave you because you'd failed by giving him a less-than-typical child? Silliness. You guys are stronger than ever.

Oscar is eager to learn, to explore, and is fiercely independent so you needn't have worried about that either. There is no such thing as conventional beauty. Oscar is perfect to you.

There are challenges in raising him but the love far, far outweighs anything that crops up. You'll learn as much about yourself, as you will about Oscar. You shouldn't have underestimated yourself. You're coping just fine. Oh and you should never have underestimated him. Oscar surprises you every day with his strength and determination.

The milestones? So they might take a little longer to grasp. But when he does, my goodness, they are the most memorable, most magical moments.

Children with Down syndrome have meaningful relationships with their siblings. Oscar's relationship with his brother is exactly how you imagined it would be before you learnt your son had Down syndrome.

So life, without question or doubt, is better with Oscar in it. I promise you. Oh and a final note and just for the record—"Sometimes the things you were most afraid of, turn out to be the things that make you the happiest."

Love, Me (today) X

Life in abundance comes only through great love.

Elbert Hubbard

That Extra Something

Starr Ayers
Asheboro, North Carolina

"Your baby has Down syndrome!"

Surely our physician was mistaken. I'd just held her.

Hadn't I marveled at her strength as she lifted her tiny head from my shoulder? Hadn't I unwrapped the pink flannel blanket to reveal all seven pounds of wrinkly flesh and counted every last finger and toe for myself?

Our child was nothing less than perfect!

Life seldom unfolds as we expect. Yet, in the unexpected we gain a greater understanding of God's love. It is there we learn.

Our daughter may fall short of people's expectations, but in the eyes of her Creator, she is perfect. Knit in the secret place by the hands of the One who knows no imperfection, she is fearfully and wonderfully made and perfect for the role she was created to play in our lives.

For you formed my inward parts;
  you knitted me together in my mother's womb.
I praise you, for I am fearfully and wonderfully made.
Wonderful are your works;
  my soul knows it very well.
My frame was not hidden from you,
when I was being made in secret,
  intricately woven in the depths of the earth.
Your eyes saw my unformed substance;
in your book were written, every one of them,
  the days that were formed for me,
  when as yet there was none of them.
  – Psalm 139:13±16, ESV

Less than perfect? Hardly. Instead, our daughter has that little something extra. Intricately woven within every cell of her body is an extra copy of the twenty-first chromosome.

I'd say that makes her extra special. Wouldn't you?

Every single person is sacred. Sacred means special, precious, a treasure of true beauty. That means you.

Amy Leigh Mercree

What a Difference a Day Makes

Starr Ayers
Asheboro, North Carolina

When my daughter was small, she would always get up in the morning and look out the window to see if the sun was shining.

I called her "my sunshine girl."

She still is.

She loved the musical *Annie* and the song "Tomorrow."

She still does.

When I was sad, she could always lift me up.

She still can.

She would pat me softly on the shoulder and say, "Don't worry, Mommy. It'll be all right. The sun'll come out tomorrow."

It always did.

May your day be filled with sunshine. And if not today, look outside tomorrow.

Perhaps, the sun'll come out.

It always does!

Today's limits will be tomorrow's victories.

Danielle Orner

Paths

Sue Bessell
Bristol, England

I'm of the belief that no two stories are the same. We are all individuals and it shouldn't matter whether we have a disability or not.

That's one of the reasons I cringe when I hear people talk about the limitations of Down syndrome. We have never placed limitations on our son; those have been placed there by a society that can't see past the condition. I prefer to celebrate the individual, an individual with the abilities to go far, achieve great things, and to surprise many with their accomplishments . . . our son has done all of this and more in his thirty years of being with us.

The individual in my case is my son Nathan, born on February 21, 1985. Nathan was our fifth child, and he was born with Down syndrome. June 1987 would see the arrival of his younger sibling Madison. Nathan now had two brothers and three sisters, and he is very much a part of a very loving family.

When Nathan was fifteen I managed to find him a place with a drama company, and his love of entertaining blossomed. It was when Nathan was around the age of twenty-five that the idea of writing a play about his childhood came about, and the play *Up Down Boy* was developed, with Nathan playing himself. The play took off and was a success. It was put on at many venues around the country over three years, and we were very excited to have been asked to perform the play at The National Theatre London in their venue The Shed. We also had the most wonderful opportunity to take the play to New Zealand. My son indeed took me to the other side of the world and back again.

Nathan is and always has been a pure source of joy. He is a wonderful person to be with and you can't fail to be won over by his happy and delightful nature. Life's not always been easy, of course it hasn't, but the good times most certainly outweigh the bad.

Would I change anything about my son? No, not one hair on his head would I want changed.

 For more about *Up Down Boy*, visit www.nationaltheatre.org.uk/shows/up-down-boy.

What makes you different . . . inspires others . . .
let it shine . . . and inspire yourself.

Camilla Downs

My Precious Child

Sue Bessell
Bristol, England

Today a miracle has taken place.
And as I look into your beautiful face
I find it's very hard to believe
You are not the same as the others I see.

Something inside – it can't be seen.
It's left you different so it seems.
But for a fold. A crease. A line.
All kinds of things running through my mind.

But as I watch you grow from babe to man
I pray that you will understand
It's not the difference that I see
But all the love you give to me.

So come my child – take my hand.
We will begin life's journey on this land.
For you to me are like no other,
My precious child always.
I will be proud to say I am your mother.

All you need is love. Love is all you need.

The Beatles

Each Other

Teresa Eaton
Riverside, California

My reason to smile is that I am Ricky's Mom. He is sweet, gentle, loves babies, and enjoys music to the fullest! He loves his brothers and his niece and new-phews. He has taught me so much, and I thank God I'm his mother.

It makes me smile when I see Ricky's patience; he has been through heart surgery, pneumonia, bronchitis, long stays at the hospital, and has never once complained! Several years ago, I learned that he had a more serious illness. After the shock of learning what was ahead for my son, I was told that I would have to administer shots to him for the next six months, three times a week. He saw me get very upset and he looked at me and very gently placed his hand on mine, telling me: "That's okay Mom, don't cry!"

The next day, a nurse taught me how to give him the shot. I couldn't help but burst into tears, as I thought of the pain that I would be inflicting on him. As I turned to Ricky, I saw my son looking at me, smiling, as he lifted his t-shirt and pinched the spot where I had to inject him. "Mom, it's okay. See? You can do it, here! I will hold my belly for you!"

I smiled and gave him the shot. He endured the shots and the side effects for six months! He lost hair, lost weight, had frequent headaches, but yet, never one complaint! He taught me to be strong for him, to have faith that everything had a reason and he would get better.

My son has given me many reasons to smile over the years, through milestones he has reached and the funny things he has done. For example, when he was fourteen years old, he locked himself in his room with his electric razor and came out "brow-less," with a huge hairline and no sideburns, as well as no hair on one arm! We had to go the doctor that day and the look on everyone when they saw Ricky coming in was unforgettable! Ricky never touched another electric razor, until the day he asked me to do his sideburns!

I thank God for him. He is my companion, my support, my shoulder to cry on sometimes, my food critic, my movie partner, and I am so proud and honored that I was chosen to be his mom. I'm here for him, and he is here for me too . . . unconditionally! Well, until he marries his girlfriend, he says. Then he will move out and I can go visit them!

I am elated that I found a book where we can share our children's achievements, or just talk about our pride and joy that we have for our children as well as the feeling of being a part of something wonderful that belongs to all us parents, families and caregivers for children with special needs. We are a part of each other.

Love does not consist in gazing at each other, but in looking outward together in the same direction.

Antoine de Saint-ExupÉry

Love Each New Experience

Thomas Pellinger
Berlin, Maryland

The first time we saw a Doppler ultrasound image of our son's face, he made us smile. And at just eighteen months of age, Conor has inspired thousands more smiles.

The odds were against Conor being born. Just weeks after we learned that we were pregnant with twin boys, prenatal tests indicated that it was highly probable Conor had Down syndrome. Shortly thereafter, we learned that Conor had hydrocephalus, a condition characterized by excess cerebrospinal fluid within the ventricles of the brain. This excess fluid put pressure on Conor's developing brain tissue and caused his head to increase in size at a more rapid than normal rate. This combination was dangerous, drastically reducing his chances of a live birth. To make matters more complicated, since Conor's head was larger than typical, the boys had to be delivered several weeks early, via a caesarean birth.

On the morning of March 15, 2013, Conor entered the world, two minutes after his brother, Will. On just his second day of life, Conor underwent brain surgery to insert a shunt, to drain the excess fluid from his brain. He spent several months in the hospital, to heal and let his premature body develop and grow. At ten months old, Conor returned to the hospital to have his tonsils and adenoids removed. The surgery made it painful for Conor to swallow and left our normally happy son crying in our arms all night.

Throughout these ordeals, Conor has shown remarkable resilience. He sees Will do things that he cannot yet achieve and sometimes this seems to frustrate him. Yet, he pushes on, despite his lower muscle tone, increased joint laxity, and heavier head. He strains his way through his physical therapy exercises. He says new words at first in a whisper, his volume growing with his confidence. And with each new accomplishment, he flashes his brilliant smile and shares his infectious laugh.

When we learned we were having twin boys, we thought a lot about the things we would teach them. How to ride a bike, read a book, use power tools. We soon discovered that each day was a new learning experience for us as well. Conor has already taught us valuable lessons. He has taught us to appreciate the tranquility of sitting together quietly, as he studies our faces with his perceptive blue eyes. He has taught us a depth of empathy we have never known. When he detects a look of pain or sadness, his expression changes to that of concern, with lower lip protruded, and he reaches his tiny hands out to gently touch our faces. Most of all, Conor has taught us to genuinely love each new experience, as much as we love him.

Empathy is about finding echoes of another person in yourself.

mohsin hamid

Blessed

Tracy Bryon
Edgemead, Cape Town, South Africa

Robyn gives us reasons to laugh or smile daily. She has a great sense of humour, loves to imitate, and has given us many special memories.

She was three or four years old and we were waiting at the audiologist for her check-up. An elderly person walking with the aid of a walking stick entered the reception area and hobbled along to a seat. Robyn got up on her feet, walked very slowly, and limped across the room. She kept going until she walked straight into the door, head down, and then fell onto her back with her feet in the air. This little antic had everyone in hysterics.

More recently, her older brother took part in a karate competition. The only people allowed on the mat were the competitors and referees. There had been a break in the fight, everyone was called to the judges' table, and I was distracted. I then heard laughter and looked up. Robyn was on the mat, not too well coordinated and having a "fight" with an imaginary opponent.

This child of ours enjoys life. In spite of some real difficulties and health challenges that she's experienced, she still smiles, finds joy in the most mundane, and laughs heartily. She is determined to make the most of her capabilities.

She strives to be independent. When she started going to a mainstream school in a special program, she was totally excited to be able to wear a school uniform. She mostly likes to get homework; she is enjoying reading and improves weekly. She wants to write shopping lists, read them back, buy the groceries, and then pay for them.

Robyn finds pleasure in helping in the kitchen and loves to bake. It really is a help having someone to cut the vegetables or salads, cheerfully. She can fry an egg, make school lunches, and make a cup of tea or coffee. She will wash dishes, but it isn't really her favourite chore. She prefers to take washing off the line, folding it so neatly.

We have a swimming pool at home so learning to swim was really "not negotiable." It helped that Robyn loves the water—she was "water safe" for a long time before a reasonable stroke developed. Then she was selected to swim in the school gala. Her brother is a swimmer and so she once again imitated; we saw her with goggles on, a towel rolled under her arm and walking so proudly to the pool area. She didn't win the little race that day, but we saw that years of swimming lessons had paid off. She had her moment of glory. She participated and enjoyed the experience.

I think Robyn has an outlook on life that we can all learn from—find joy in the little things, laugh often, love a lot, and embrace life. We are blessed to have her as our daughter.

Just keep swimming!

Dory

Tandem

Deborah Leigh Norman
Fort Wayne, Indiana

I saw a couple riding a tandem bike today. For me, seeing a tandem is a good reminder that I need to stop only looking at what is yet to be accomplished and that I should occasionally look at how far we have come.

My older son learned to ride a bike when he was four years old, and by then my younger son who has Down syndrome had just turned one and could sit in a carrier on the back of my bike. Day trips, vacations, or just around town, we would ride our bikes often, and enjoyed family time exploring new areas from a perspective different than a car and covering more ground than we could by walking.

Back then when I saw a tandem, I would think, "Well, if he never learns to ride a bike, a tandem is another way we could still enjoy riding as a family."

When my son outgrew the carrier, we moved him to an attachment behind my bike. Continuing the progression, I bought a balance bike and a bike with training wheels. Then I attached a handle to his bike and took off the training wheels. This handle was the best tool toward him learning to ride. After a long time, I was able to let go for a few seconds. Eventually the length of time grew and he reached eight seconds, seventeen, thirty, a minute, two minutes, until he learned to ride independently.

The progression didn't stop there, however. He had to learn steering and braking. He had to learn how to get started by himself and ride up and down the driveway. Next was learning how to ride a bike with gears.

This long process is similar to many things my son with Down syndrome has achieved, such as walking, potty training, putting on and zipping his coat, and much more. He did it, but it took a long time and it made us break down into small steps how, for example, to "ride a bike." This is hard work that requires much patience, but each step completed is a celebration and it makes the effort worth it.

My son loves riding his bike. When the kids see him riding to school in the morning, they see him as just another kid on a bike, and some are impressed that he can do something that they can't yet.

Now when I see a tandem I smile and think of our long process. I am reminded of how my son with Down syndrome helps me to appreciate the many steps that go into learning something new and to savor the accomplishment in a whole new way with a whole new joy.

If we ever get a tandem it may be my husband and me riding it, like that couple I saw today. Or maybe I can ride with my son sitting up front and he can show me new things to enjoy along the way, like he always does.

Every child is gifted. They just unwrap
their packages at different times.

Unknown

Wonderful World

Barbara Roussel
Mandeville, Louisiana

My son Simon sees the world through rose-colored lenses. When he sings Louis Armstrong's "What a Wonderful World," motioning "trees of green" and "skies of blue" in sign language, he is singing about his life.

Simon had been football manager and unofficial "assistant coach" for eight years, throughout junior high and high school. Before and after every game, he loved to fire up the team with a pep talk. It didn't matter that the other players couldn't understand his words; they understood his enthusiasm and always emerged from their huddle cheering and smiling.

An hour before the last game of Simon's senior year, the head coach asked him if he wanted to "dress out." He had never before worn pads or even a helmet.

After years of happily watching on the sidelines, Simon suited up for the first time, donning the #5 jersey and joined the guys for warm-up exercises as if he had been training for years.

The game started and a teammate caught the kickoff ball and handed it to Simon. Cradling the ball, Simon took off down the field, protected by his teammates. The announcer called the play yard by yard, his voice rising in pitch as the crowd roared and cheered. Simon broke free of the protective wall formed by his teammates, sprinting into the end zone. He scored a touchdown!

This special play was captured on film by a local sportscaster. The touchdown went viral and became the lead story on Yahoo.com. A feature story on the local TV news about Simon and his high school experience won an Associated Press award. A radio show 1,300 miles away featured the story on their "good news" reports. Strangers, a year later, approach Simon regularly and ask him if he was the boy whom they saw score the touchdown.

Back at school, as always, Simon greeted everyone as his friend. At the homecoming dance and at prom, he was the first one on the dance floor and the last to leave. On the marathon senior Disney trip, he kept up with everyone at all the parks. At the overnight graduation party, he watched the sun come up.

And of course, he went back to giving his famous pep talks: as manager of the basketball team, Simon inspired his team all the way to the playoffs.

For a graduation gift, Simon received an album filled with letters from students, coaches, teachers, and administrators telling him how much he inspired them and thanking him for his support and dedication. Some former students even mailed letters to him from college.

My son is my biggest inspiration. I look at him and the amazing things he has accomplished and I think to myself what a wonderful world it is indeed.

Optimism is the faith that leads to achievement.
Nothing can be done without hope and confidence.

Helen Keller

Do You Need a Hug?

Debra Dittmar
New Hope, Pennsylvania

It was February 2002 when Cameron, my dad, and I were driving from New Hope, Pennsylvania, to Hurricane, West Virginia, for a family funeral. This trip was a very long drive and to make matters worse the weather was bad, rain, sleet, and snow! As we neared the top of the mountain pass, we saw a sign for McDonald's at the next exit. Cameron clapped with joy hoping for a chocolate milkshake.

It was crazy inside the McDonald's! Everyone on the highway must have stopped. All registers were open and each line was packed. As was our custom, I asked Cameron which line he wanted to order from. He chose the one with the pretty blond-haired girl. The lines were long and moving slowly. As we stood waiting, Cameron was busy looking at everyone. He turned to face me and planted a wet sloppy kiss on my check. Then in his way, Cameron wriggled around to be facing outward. We all took one step closer to the counter to place our order.

At that moment, Cameron decided to reach out to the woman in front of us. He grabbed her left shoulder and pulled her around to face him. The face and eyes of anger met both Cameron's eyes and mine! I thought to myself, "Please don't let Cameron upset this woman!" At that exact moment, Cameron opened his arms up and said, "Hug?" And then he looked at me. I politely said that Cameron would like to give her a hug and would that be okay? She nodded okay, but seemed a little hesitant. My next hope was that it would be the "short" hug and not the "long" one. Cameron latched on to this woman and gave her a very big bear hug that went on for several minutes. Cameron's face was looking at me and the woman was facing the other direction. After what seemed like an eternity, the hug was over and Cameron wanted his "mommy" back. When the woman turned around to pass Cameron back to me her eyes seemed to fade away into pools of darkness. The "hug" was over. The woman looked at me then said, "I can't remember the last time anyone hugged me! Thank you Cameron!" With that the woman wiped away her tears and moved forward to place her order. As usual, I'm not sure who learned more that day. Me or the other woman with the sad eyes.

Now, as then, whenever Cameron says "Hug?" I look at the person, and explain that Cameron would like to pass along a hug! After the hug is over, there is usually some brief story that the person shares, or they have a loved one with special needs. Whatever the reason, God has decided that Cameron will pass along hugs to the first person he comes in contact with for the day, or the 101st person. Cameron and "God" seem to know when someone needs a special hug!

We shall never know all the good
that a simple smile can do.

Mother Teresa

Darling Natalia

Hayley Goleniowska
Cornwall, England

Your name means birth and Christmas, for that is when you arrived in our lives.

You came a little early, and oh, what an entrance you made.

Blue and silent, so small and beautifully fragile . . . our scrubbed bathroom floor was where we first met. I was frozen with shock and sick with worry, but you certainly grabbed our attention.

In those early weeks your determination became clear as we let the diagnosis sink in. You hung between worlds, clinging to life, and your purpose had already begun. We learnt that life cannot be planned, boxes ticked, and crucially, that what will enrich our lives is not necessarily the path we would think to choose.

Unaware of the stigma attached to that extra chromosome of yours, you were simply our precious baby daughter first and foremost. I am sorry it took us a while to forget the symptoms and predictions, but you showed us never to take anything for granted.

Right from the first days, our expectations for you were high. We persevered with expressing and didn't stop until you had learnt your first life skill at three months old, to nurse your mother's milk. You have gone on to survive keyhole heart surgery and countless ills that sent us dashing to the hospital at all hours of day and night. But somehow you always mustered a smile, or a cheeky raspberry blow, to dissolve the tension of a fellow patient, parent, or tired staff member.

You have melted hearts and changed perceptions wherever you go. And yes, you have opened doors and broken down barriers in the media and advertising world. You have drawn in the masses and melted myths with your diva ways.

Your smile means so much to many as it beams down from a billboard, as you continue to change the face of beauty in advertising. It shouts for all to hear that your life is worth living, and that you are living it to the full. It shows beyond doubt that we all have a place, a worth, a purpose. It is inclusion at its best.

But more than that, you are creating tiny ripples of change with each and every ordinary day. The intuitive hug for a cancer patient in our local doctor's surgery, the way you dissipate a squabble between two boys in the schoolyard, a kissed knee when a friend falls. The teacher who has learnt a new way of conveying his message, the proud grandparent, the younger classmate you read to who will grow up without ignorance. An annoyed big sister you have carefully played just so, or an exasperated parent you have led a merry dance. Yes, you are just like the rest of the gang.

For we are all unique and colourful in our ways, just as we are all more alike than not. That December we were given an incredible gift, a second precious daughter to cherish with all our hearts.

See the light in others, and treat them as if that is all you see.

Dr. Wayne Dyer

No Boundaries

Heather Boyd
Celina, Texas

My reason to smile decided to make his appearance ten weeks early on Christmas Day in 2008. We knew that Max had Down syndrome, but what we did not know was how much our tiny three-pound baby was going to change our lives. Max looked up at me with those gorgeous, baby blue eyes and the world stopped. I knew at that moment we were going to get through this. There is something absolutely magical about Max. As we watched Max go through sixteen weeks in the NICU, multiple surgeries, g-tube, and tons of doctor appointments, he never skipped a beat. Every nurse, doctor, person in the waiting room, grocery store, and church felt the warmth Max brought to the room. Six years later, he continues to shine and amaze us daily!

Max started kindergarten recently, and as any mother experiencing this exciting time would agree, I was full of mixed emotions. Was this the right school for Max? What modifications were needed, if any? Millions of questions were running through my mind. Max started kindergarten and hasn't looked back since. He's thrived in the school setting, reading sight words, writing his full name and words, and he has more friends than I can count! Quick trips to the grocery store turn into play dates because around every aisle is another friend excited to see him! At the time I was so worried about the "what ifs" I should have known that Max has no boundaries. Every child will face inevitable challenges, but it is the grace and determination that defines them. Max's grace and determination set examples for his younger brother and sister, as well as for our entire family.

I came across a quote once that said, "Down syndrome happens randomly, like flipping a coin or winning the lottery." I believe 110% that I am the luckiest lottery winner ever! The power he holds in his smile is immeasurable. He meets every challenge and milestone in front of him in stride. He is kind, charismatic, smart, beautiful, determined, funny, and above all, the most loving child. Max loves with everything he has in him. He has a sixth sense for people's emotions and knows that reaching out to hold your hand does more than words. I am blessed beyond belief to be the mother of this amazing little boy. I never could have imagined the beautiful change our lives experienced the day Max was born. I can hardly wait to see what my little boy has in store for this world. Believe me, there are no boundaries!

When I started counting my blessings,
my whole life turned around.

Willie Nelson

Proms Are Fun

Jillian Berube
Westminster, Massachusetts

When I was in high school I could not wait for the prom! When the time came, I loved shopping for a new dress and then taking some pictures and sending them to my friends. My cousin did my hair, put on my makeup, and added some bling. I put on my dress.

At the prom, I felt pretty amazing and elegant wearing my simple black dress. The music was too loud, but it did not bother me. I felt beautiful! It was so much fun because I got picked for the princess court! I was shocked to hear my name called! I didn't think they would call me for the court. When I was picked for the princess court I had to choose someone to dance with. I got to dance with my long-time crush, and I felt extra special. When we were dancing, someone took a picture of us, and it ended up being printed in the yearbook. All night, I danced with my friends, took tons of pictures, and laughed. Leaving the prom that night, I didn't want it to end. After the prom was over, I took off my high-heel shoes. It felt so good to take them off!

Being in the princess court I learned something I didn't know about myself. I used to be shy and afraid, but being a part of the princess court made me realize I am not invisible. Being picked for the princess court inspired me to help other people with and without disabilities enjoy going to proms, because it can make other people feel special too.

I am now planning proms with a close friend. I help to select a theme for each prom every year. We plan the music, where it will be, the meal, the decorations, and we do a head count so everyone can have a seat. I try to include old and new friends alike. It is not that hard for me to include everyone in on the fun, because I want everyone to feel special. And our friendship and fun goes on long after the night is over.

When I think about proms with my friends, I think we'll always have a lot of fun together and take lots of pictures to capture memories that will last us forever. I always want everyone to have a fun experience and to have memories to look back on with a smile. From my experiences of planning and attending proms, everybody gets a chance to feel special when they are wearing a crown or tiara. People with and without disabilities can enjoy time with friends. Everybody gets the chance to be king or queen!

Let us be grateful to people who make us happy; they are the charming gardeners who make our souls blossom.

Marcel Proust

Three-Point Shots

Dorothy Grow
Bensalem, Pennsylvania

Kevin's story starts with one man: a teacher, a coach, a mentor, a friend. A person willing to take a chance. But to Coach John Mullin, it wasn't about taking a chance. It was a natural progression of the bond he shares with Kevin. In middle school, Kevin expressed an interest to be involved with the basketball team as manager. When he started high school, Coach Mullin—who also happened to be his teacher— reached out to him to join the varsity team as the manager. For four years, Kevin attended every practice and game. The team embraced him and treated him like "one of the guys." Starting in freshman year, practice didn't end until Kevin made the final free throw. Sometimes he made it . . . and sometimes he missed. But the team never complained as they ran "suicides" until he finally made his shot.

Near the end of basketball season of Kevin's senior year, Coach Mullin told us he intended to "suit Kevin up" for the final game of the season. As his parents, this was a dream come true. We knew Kevin would be thrilled, and for us, it was a chance to see our son in a varsity uniform . . . more than we ever expected.

With the "ceremonial" shot out of the way, and the team with a comfortable lead, both coaches agreed to have Kevin go back in the game during the final two minutes. What happened next turned Kevin's world upside down. Four out of five three-point shots led to instant fame. The next month was a whirlwind! There were national news stories, a two-day contract with the Philadelphia 76ers, and a chance to meet his dream team, the Harlem Globetrotters, at a school-wide assembly, and an opportunity to play with the team.

His school community produced a documentary, *Kevin's Story*, which won best documentary at Greenfield Film Festival (www.bit.ly/KevinGrowsStory). We are truly blessed to be part of a community that has embraced our family.

Kevin's dad summed up the whole experience. During an interview he shared a really thoughtful statement: "We all expected to discuss how this changed Kevin, and it hasn't changed Kevin. The questions is, how did it change us?"

For us, this was an opportunity for awareness . . . we are so grateful to be able to share Kevin's story, and his smile, with so many.

Never give up, for that is just the place
and time that the tide will turn.

Harriet Beecher Stowe

Changing the World

Teresa Renee
Santa Cruz, California

We sat high up in the stands watching the Homecoming celebration unfold on the field during Brandon's freshman year of high school. The usual kids were on display and the crowd was awaiting the announcement of the king and queen. Brandon was on the edge of his seat awaiting word of the winners. It was at this moment he turned to me and said, "I want to be the Homecoming king when I am a senior." Little did we know that this impossible dream ultimately turned Brandon into the game changer at a place where they've been playing by the same rules for over forty years. Rules that didn't include electing young adults like Brandon as Homecoming king.

He was set on his goal even when others didn't share his vision. As parents, it was painful to watch because we knew the reality. It simply wasn't possible because he was the student who only got to watch others celebrate their achievements. Achievements reserved for the in-crowd, the popular kids. He persevered by dressing up solo on spirit days and jumping into the Homecoming parade without a formal role or place. He created his own space in the line-up and danced his heart out. He had fun regardless. He chose his own path of inclusion. Brandon didn't care what others thought and didn't ever see limits.

As his parents, we tried to temper him at times when his dreams appeared too lofty. This was one of them. After three difficult years of Brandon being blocked from many opportunities, he took it into his own hands and said to us, "I'm going to blow up my senior year." I heard him say under his breath, "I really want to be part of Homecoming this year." We thought he meant being in the skit or helping to assemble the float, but he had other aspirations and became his own advocate to get into Associated Student Body Leadership. The beauty in his quest was he wanted ASB Leadership not entirely for his gain but to help others who were on the outside looking in.

When he told us that he was accepted into ASB Leadership, we knew the winds of change were in motion. We knew that this Homecoming season was going to be different for him and his classmates. Not only was he able to be part of assembling the float, he was also on the back of a convertible as one of the five elected couples in the Homecoming court. Brandon was crowned Homecoming king, winning the popular vote of the school!

Just like he predicted, he did blow up during his senior year. But it didn't stop at Homecoming. His crown was the launching pad for his foundation 321Life+1, which he created to help others have an inclusive school experience. He knows what it's like to feel excluded and isolated, so now he's changing and inspiring . . . one person at a time!

 For more on Brandon's foundation, visit www.321life.com.

We must become the change we
wish to see in the world.

Mahatma gandhi

The Three-Winged Butterfly

Lindsey Kelley
Kearney, Nebraska

A caterpillar inched his way until it was his special day
To cuddle up, to patiently wait, for Mother Nature to create
But from his bundle
(to our surprise)
He was slower to rise than other butterflies.
Our heart first felt sadness
At what we did see
When we saw he had not two wings, but three
He bravely opened his wings
And shone his colors so bright
. . . then he smiled
To tell us everything was all right.
With each flutter, each folly, each fall,
He seemed to get up
Standing twice as tall!
He painted the sky
With the boldest of colors
As he dipped
And he dove
And he swooped
And he fluttered
We understand now
It became quite clear
His differences were beautiful
And nothing to fear.
We opened our hearts
We surrounded him and loved him
And promised
He would never have to fly alone
In the sky above him.
Now we fly with full hearts
And we swoop
And we sweep
All because he never gave up
And neither did we.

We delight in the beauty of the butterfly,
but rarely admit the changes it has gone
through to achieve that beauty.

Maya Angelou

Anything Can Happen, If You Let It

Mardra Sikora
Omaha, Nebraska

A few years ago, Caroline Sheen, the actress playing Mary Poppins in the Broadway Across America cast, sang "Anything Can Happen If You Let It" on Omaha's Orpheum Theatre stage, while Marcus sat backstage in his "kite boy" costume, alternately listening and chatting with the cast while waiting for his scene.

I was lucky enough to be sitting next to him while the touring Broadway professionals danced on and off the stage, sharing laughter and stories with Marcus between costume changes.

The opportunity to play a walk-on role within the touring Broadway cast came about because of an auction fundraiser for the chance to "Be on Stage with the Mary Poppins Cast," and Marcus's family and friends rallied together to "win."

That night as he walked the stage and sang with the cast, he was, in fact, doing just what Mary Poppins said: "Life is out there waiting, so go and get it." A lesson he has never needed to be taught.

Marcus dreams of creating and starring in his own Broadway musical, a dream that began long before that magical night and only grows. They say you should visualize your goals in completion. He seems to know this, as he stood in front of an empty poster frame outside the local theatre, gave me the thumbs-up, and told me, "This spot is for the *Marcus the Musical* poster."

The burdens of official training in the areas of playwriting, acting, stagecraft, and so on, do not daunt him. Non-issues. Last year Marcus told the actor who played Arthur in a community theatre's production of *Spamalot*, "I am going to play Arthur!"

The actor responded by saying, "The greatest of journeys begins with one step."

That's right. As long as you are moving forward toward your dream, you are that much closer to it. Another twenty-four-year-old without training and facing the uphill, dare I say impossible, mountain of learning and struggle, would likely give up. In fact, many young people are talked out of their dreams and move on because they "know better."

He's already taken the first step; after all, he was on stage with a touring Broadway cast. Each week he attends voice lessons with a music therapist and when the budget allows, he takes acting classes. Since his exciting night on stage he has written a one-act play that was produced in a local high school, and just recently published his first storybook for children. After the Mary Poppins night a reporter called it a "once in a lifetime" experience, but in our house we called it "just the beginning." Broadway, here we come!

 Follow Marcus's journey at GrownUpsandDowns.com and facebook.com/GrownUpsAndDowns. Learn more about Marcus' book at BlackDayBook.com.

The journey of a thousand miles
begins with one step.

Lao Tzu

Unexpected Trip to Holland

Shannon Banchero
Northville, Michigan

They say your wedding day and the birth of your children are some of the best days of your life. I have found that to be true. My wedding day, the birth of my first son, and the first half hour after my second was born were the happiest moments of my life.

Then the moment paused. The pediatrician examining my son said she had a few concerns: the extra folds around his almond-shaped eyes, the straight-lined crease on his hands, the hypotonia.

My baby boy has Down syndrome.

Blood is drawn. An echocardiogram performed. A social worker visits. Another pediatrician confirms the preliminary diagnosis. I want everyone to leave and let me sleep so I can wake up from this dream.

As I held him, he looked straight into my eyes, as if he were looking straight into my soul. From that first moment I held him I was completely and utterly in love. I knew I would do everything in my power to be a strong advocate for him.

Less than two days after his arrival, we were discharged. I decided to take him for a walk around the Labor and Delivery Ward to show him off. As I walked along, I passed a young man sweeping the floor. He stopped to tell me "Congratulations."

He had Down syndrome.

As I turned the corner I broke into tears. It's terrible to say, but it's true. You see, my boys were going to be all-American, well-rounded quarterbacks—look out Peyton and Eli! I had laid out their future before one was born and before the other was two. But none of my visions had one pushing a broom around a hospital. I was mourning the loss of the child I had expected. And that was OK.

Once I collected myself, I continued on my walk. I ran into the young man for a second time. I was mad at God; how much more "in-my-face about the future" did he have to be? The young man asked about my baby. Then he congratulated me again, looked at my baby, and said, "He's beautiful . . . he looks like me." I swallowed back the tears and thanked him for his kind words.

Beautiful. Like me.

He seemed to be referring to not only my son's sweet face, but also his own inner beauty. He didn't see the bleakness I saw. He saw a newborn, not Down syndrome. It's a gift far greater than tossing a football in the NFL to look at oneself and see the beauty and not get hung up on what society deems beautiful and typical.

My mother's intuition tells me that my son will teach more than I will have ever expected. There will be struggles. There will be tough times. This world can be a cruel place. But something tells me the joys are going to be beyond my comprehension.

Joy is the simplest form of gratitude.

Karl Barth

Tena

Monika Kajić
Jaruge, Croatia

Tena is a young adult who hides her strength in her diversity without comparing herself to others. Tena's spirit and pure soul are intact. As her primary school teacher, I enjoy recognizing the uniqueness and inexhaustible value of my students. Here's a little bit about Tena—about the full life behind this illustration.

Tena enjoys every second of her life. Her heart is big. Often, she tells me she loves her boyfriend, whom she cannot imagine her life without! She also has a knack for rhythm and music; she always has a place of honor as singer and entertainer when hanging out with her friends.

Tena is a member of several associations in neighboring cities that promote equality and togetherness among children. She travels to the sea with them and goes to numerous gatherings that are invaluable to her. Lately, she says she wants to be a pastry chef because she loves making cakes with her mother. She finds the recipes herself and has developed a love for food preparation and baking.

While her parents are at work, Tena stays home alone. She is very aware of the love her parents give her, and she appreciates it. She often thanks God for all she has, and finds comfort in prayer. She enjoys reading and writing too. She holds a special place in her heart for poetry. In fact, she bought my heart with her poetry many years ago, and she is still working on her craft to this day. Reading her poems—rich in rhyme and emotion—causes tears to well up in my eyes. Hearing her poetry, I realize differences are what make us unique and that we are miraculously created in the image of God.

I drew a portrait of Tena when she was my student. I just loved her smile. Sometimes, her smile made my hardworking days the best days possible. Every time I look at this portrait I drew with love, I have one thousand reasons to smile and one thousand reasons to have a nice day, and one thousand words cannot describe the happiness and satisfaction of the teaching profession that allows me to get to know the children and their worlds. All children are equal, and Tena helped me realize that.

Watching Tena's life unfold has also showed me that roles can be reversed. My little student grew into a beautiful woman and became a great life teacher to me and everyone around us.

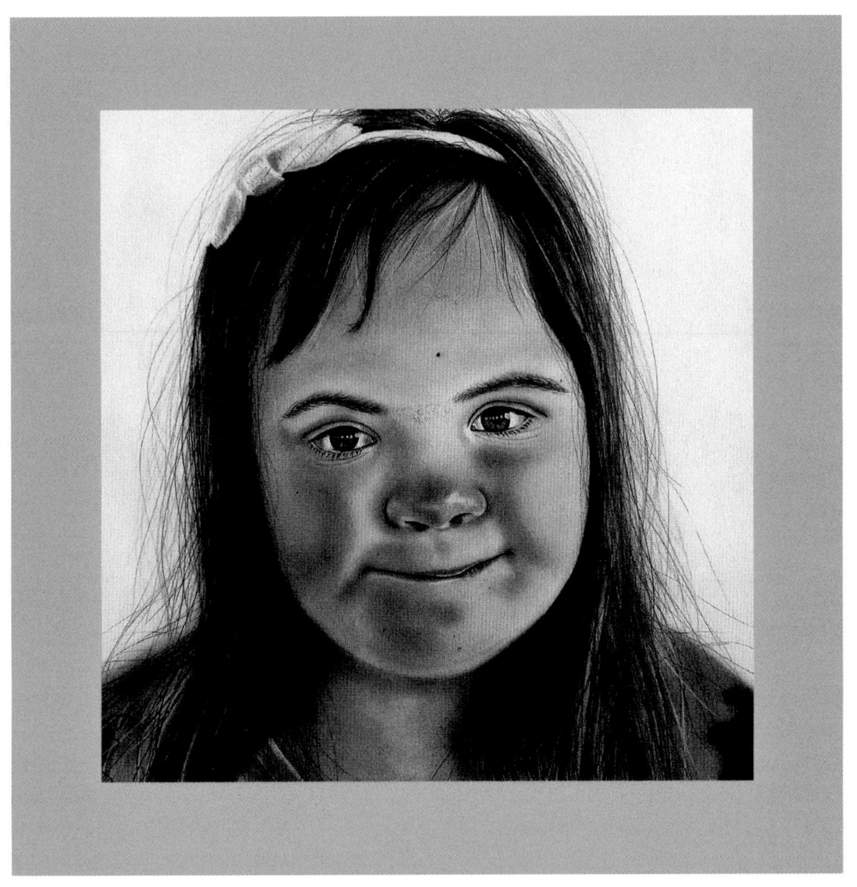

If a child cannot learn in the way we teach . . .
we must teach in a way the child can learn.

Dr. o. ivar lovaas

Aimee

Aimee Connolly
Dublin, Ireland

One of my memories of when I was small, is listening to the soft mellow sounds of my xylophone. I remember Easter egg hunts where my dad and mum hid chocolate eggs around the garden. The xylophone helped me find the eggs before our little dog could sniff them out! When I was far away from the hidden eggs, Mum played a low note slowly; as I got closer, the notes became faster and higher in pitch! This was probably my very first music lesson!

Some people expect I won't play well just because I have Down syndrome. So I love to surprise them!

The main instruments I play are tin whistle, flute, harp, and bodhrλn. I love to play traditional Irish. I have about 100 tunes learned, all in my head! I've composed ten or twelve traditional-style tunes of my own and have even performed some of them on TV and on radio.

One ambition I have had for a while is to hear my compositions performed by a favourite musician. This ambition came true just recently! I was invited to a party (at the Mexican Ambassador's residence) in Dublin. I was asked by the host to play some tunes for the guests, which I did, and I finished off with one of my own compositions.

Paddy Moloney (of The Chieftains) was among the guests. He took out his whistle and said, "Play that again, AimPe, and I'll play it back to ye!" So the two of us together played a duet of my tune, *The Birds Are Singing*, and everyone cheered!

Through Down Syndrome Ireland, I received the most amazing job of my life! In 2010 I auditioned for the part of voice-over artist for Punky. Punky is the main character in the animation series produced by Geronimo Productions and now shown on RTE Junior. I'll never forget the day I got the phone call to say I'd got the part! I was totally thrilled! I love the character of Punky, with her funny ways and her quirky ideas. It feels like she is part of me and will be forever.

I'm just finishing a two-year course in Performing Arts at Roslyn Park College, Dublin. It has been an incredible learning experience. I've been part of several stage performances. In my favourite performance, entitled *La Luna de Federico*, one of my parts involved singing a solo lament, in Irish. In another part I played the flute, while following choreographed movements with the other performers. We performed this play as part of the 5-Lamp Festival in Dublin without a hitch! We got great applause at the ending!

The future? I'd like to get more acting parts and voice-over work. I want to encourage more writers and directors to include parts for people with disabilities. I want to work more professionally in this area, and in music, to enjoy myself, to earn some money, and to be an independent woman.

Perseverance is not a long race. It is many short races one after another.

Walter Elliot

Togetherness

Pina Rahill
Chalfont, Pennsylvania

I didn't smile when Gianna was born. In fact, I cried, suffocated by the news that "she has characteristics of a child with Down syndrome." At the same time, I ached to hold her. When they brought her to me, I lowered all five pounds of her onto my bare chest, caressed her back, and kissed the crown of her head. "I'm sorry," I whispered, feeling like I'd given her a life that she wouldn't want.

That was ten years ago. It didn't take long, however, to see that Gianna doesn't wish for life to be any different than it is. It didn't take long for smiles to replace tears.

When Gianna was two months old, I sat on the couch with her draped over my shoulder; my oldest son, thirteen at the time, sat to my left. We mindlessly watched as the camera on *Good Morning America* panned the crowd and then rested on a young woman with Down syndrome. I wondered what thoughts might be running through my son's head—about the young woman and about his little sister. Seconds later, he held out his arms and said in that nonchalant, easy-going teenage-boy way, "Here, let me hold her." I lifted her from my shoulder and plunked her into his big hands, smiling as they swallowed her whole.

Fast forward six years. My third-oldest son who was almost seven when his little sister was born was now thirteen and playing in one of the biggest basketball games of his young career. It was a rough night for my son. He went zero for twelve shots in what was a painful loss. After the game, we waited for him outside of the gym, expecting him to walk out with shoulders hunched, eyes lowered and a gait that said, "Let's just go home." When Gianna spotted him, she ran to him and grabbed his hand. No one would have judged him harshly had he ignored her. He didn't though. He took her hand, smiled, and let himself be led to the car. His older brother, sixteen at the time, trailed them. He shook his head and said, "Gi can always get you to smile."

Most recently, my youngest son, born with a rare genetic disorder and who is Gianna's closest sibling in age called, crying frantically, while my husband and I were driving home. "I need you. I really do. Come home now," he said. I calmed him the best I could, then said, "Fran, where's Gi? How about you find Gianna and ask her for a hug?" "Okay," he said, in a voice brimming with emotion.

We see in Gianna a person who enjoys life as it is and who perhaps more readily than the rest of us recognizes what is important—love, family togetherness, and yes, a burger and fries. And because of that, we can't help but smile.

The world needs that special gift that only you have.

Marie Forleo

Faith

Lisa Wajert
Holland, Pennsylvania

When Matthew was born in March of 1990, I was newly married, twenty-three years old, and living in Massachusetts, away from my family. As shocking as it was to have a child with Down syndrome, it was even more shocking to hear the doctors in the hospital tell me, "You can just leave him here if you want. There are people who will adopt him and you can walk away and try again. After all, you are young and you can try again to have a `normal' child."

Needless to say, I could not wait to get out of there, go back to my home state of Pennsylvania, return to my family and friends, and start raising my son. Things were rough in those early years! Like many of us encounter, there were constant trips to doctors and specialists. Matthew was given a myriad of "alphabet soup" diagnoses—ADHD, ODD, etc.—and his behavioral issues were quite significant early on. Yet through it all Matthew flourished.

Today, he is twenty-four years old and the light of our lives! He works twenty-five hours a week in competitive employment at a middle school cafeteria, where he gets summers off and the chance to attend an adult day program with his friends and also relax at the Jersey shore. He is an avid Philly sports fan and especially enjoys being a Flyers season ticket holder, attending the games with his stepdad Sean.

Matt's faith has always been an important part of his life, and he has never let having Down syndrome stop him from participating in it. He has been an altar server at his local parish for over twelve years, serving for masses whenever he is called upon. He participates in helping out at the Parish Religious Education Program where I used to teach, and now he is a standard "fixture" in the program! Finally, and most importantly, in 2012 Matt became a Knight of Columbus. Currently he is a third degree, and hopes to pursue his fourth degree (we call him "Sir Matt"). Matt feels such an incredible sense of pride in serving beside his brother Knights and helping his parish in various fundraisers, which benefit our parish and local communities.

Matthew is quite an independent young man, loving son, brother, and stepbrother. He has a wicked sense of humor and makes us all laugh on a daily basis. Rarely does he have a bad day. Looking back on those early years, it is sometimes hard to imagine that this wonderful, strong, and independent young man is the same person! It's been a strange and crazy adventure . . . but one I would never change a minute of. Matthew has blessed all our lives and made us all better people for knowing him.

Be faithful in small things because it is
in them that your strength lies.

Mother Teresa

My Reason to Smile

Terry Eichhoff
Johannesburg, South Africa

It's a sweltering day today and I can hear my eight-year-old twins splashing around in the pool. Their laughter brings a smile to my face, and the journey we've travelled to get to this stage seems to be so distant.

Katelyn and Matthew are extremely close and are very supportive of each other. It is a special bond shared by so many twins. Katelyn loves to dance and sing and is the artist of the household. She is a social butterfly and her inner light shines brightly. Matthew plays soccer and tenpin bowling, swims, and loves to dance and to play dress-up with his sister. He is very friendly and melts hearts. Matthew is passionate about animals and wants to be a farmer when he grows up. Oh, did I mention that he has Down syndrome?

Only a parent of a special needs child knows what it feels like to go through the continual roller coaster of emotions, from the moment when the reality sets in after being told that one of your children has a special need or isn't "normal." What is the definition of "normal" anyway? I have a normal child with a special need who has touched the lives of so many people.

The intensive speech, occupational, and physio therapy has paid off. Matthew has just transferred from a special needs school to a remedial school and is coping extremely well. A top developmental pediatrician recently assessed him and she advised us that Matthew has "broken the mould" and is developing well academically. His speech has improved substantially which, in turn, has built up his confidence and social skills. Matthew is a well-balanced, happy "normal" boy who has an extra chromosome.

We stopped asking "Why?" many years ago and changed the question to "What can we do to assist Matthew?" Over the years we have learned to trust our instinct when making a decision or reviewing the progress made and planning the next steps. We also only use specialists who take care of Matthew as a person and not as a patient, and we are open to getting second opinions when something doesn't seem right to us.

Looking back though, it is the highlights of overcoming these challenges that we recall, not the challenges themselves. Matthew reached certain milestones before Katelyn did, which was a reminder that society tends to underestimate children with special needs.

To all the parents who are just finding out about their "special" child, understand that you are not alone and that you don't have to be alone. Also understand that the little milestones that your child reaches will bring you such intense joy that your heart will burst with pride. Understand that "normal" is just a label and means different things to different people.

Is it worth it? Absolutely!

If this message has helped you in any way, then I have another reason to smile . . .

"Normal" is a dryer setting.

Elizabeth Moon

Infinite

Samantha Ranwell
Auckland, New Zealand

My son, Calvin, was born seven weeks early and with the added surprise of having Down syndrome. I remember the day he was born so well. Those few words my husband Colin mumbled incoherently through his tears, about the doctor saying Calvin had characteristics of Down syndrome, shocked me beyond belief and I thought my world was shattered, indeed it felt like it was. I couldn't do it. How was I going to cope? Why me? What had I done wrong? We had to wait five of the longest days of our lives for the blood tests to confirm the doctor's initial diagnosis. As I waited and fell in love with a premature baby who needed me more than ever, his having Down syndrome became less important. Now, seven years later and with those foggy, scary, unsure first few days long behind me, I can say that the day he was born, a new and better version of myself was born too. I could do this, we could do this. As a family we would ride this unexpected journey together, learning as we went along.

I remember friends and family saying to me, as they often do when they aren't sure how to respond to the news that your child has Down syndrome, that very special parents are chosen for children with special needs. My response? Calvin did not come into my life because I was special and he needed me as some kind of Supermum—I needed him. I will be forever grateful that he chose me as his Mum and that he led me to realise what really matters in life. He has taught me how to be patient and slow down, to celebrate all accomplishments big and small, to never give up, to expect the unexpected, to be a less judgmental person, and most of all to feel a love I never knew I could.

Calvin has had this positive influence on all who have developed relationships with him, not only his family but friends, teachers, and the community too. He is an inspiration for all of us to do better because goodness knows he has to work really hard to achieve what the rest of us take for granted. He is his own best advocate, exceeding expectations, and he wows all of us who know him; all the while being his usual cheeky self with his mischievous sense of humour, using his many words and gestures or sometimes simply poking his tongue out at you followed by a giggle to show his disagreement.

I thank him for teaching me the most valuable life lessons, because without Calvin as my son I would be a lesser person. Nowadays, I could not imagine a life without him in it; he makes my days brighter and makes me smile every day. He gives me hundreds of reasons to smile, thousands of reasons to laugh and infinite reasons to feel proud.

Of all things love is the most potent.

Maria Montessori

My Recipe for Perfection

Angie Anderson
Smithfield, Utah

Ingredients

One round tummy
The crease across her hand
A soft little button nose
Two of the most beautiful blue eyes
Her tiny feet with the round pudgy toes
A chubby neck
Some soft wispy blond hair
A smile that can make anyone's day
The bum scoot

Directions

Combine all ingredients to make the most perfect little girl. The one we would do anything for. The one that melts our hearts and lights up a room. The one that makes us smile on even the worst of days. Our lives are better because you are in them.

You add that sweetness that makes us taste life more fully, makes us love harder, see things in a new light, and go beyond what we could have been. You were given to us as a gift. You are wise beyond your years and your eyes seem to see things in a different light.

You make friends with all those around you and even strangers stop to admire you. You live and learn in your own time and have taught us the value of patience. Because of this, every little thing you do is amazing to us. We are here to help you along your journey, and though it might not always be easy, we will be here to cheer you on. You can do anything! I can't wait to see what the future holds for you. We have seen miracles in your life already and I am sure there are more to come. You are unique and that's what we love so much about you. We love you just the way you are.

You have made our family recipe complete.

Love begins at home, and it is not how much we do, but how much love we put in the action that we do.

Mother Teresa

My Best Brother

Jenni Newbury Ross
Hillsborough, New Jersey

I don't remember life before my brother, Jason, was born. I'm sure there were moments I enjoyed being an only child, but when I was at the age of two, my brother was the perfect addition to our family.

Our childhood is a series of memories of the two of us together. Road trips on the couch with my dolls became real road trips to see specialists and therapists. Fake report cards written in crayon while I pretended to be Jason's teacher became real IEP meetings and celebrations with Jason when real report cards came home. Together we cheered each other on – in sports, in jobs, in life. I helped Jason get his first job, and he helped me create my dream one. Our lives are unmistakably intertwined, and I'm certain that is how it was meant to be.

So, at the age of twenty-five, as I began to plan my wedding, I knew right where he belonged. I suggested to Jason that he be my "Man of Honor," but he was insistent on the title of "Best Brother." We went with it, and he was thrilled.

My wedding day is one of my favorite days with Jason. He began that morning with a grand and unexpected gesture: proposing. He thought he'd give the two of us one last chance before I ran off with another man in my life.

As he walked me out for photos, Jason took a moment to step back into the role of younger brother. Parading across the field in the rain, he proceeded to tell me my dress was quite "bushy" and maybe I should have rethought my outfit.

In the moments I needed him most—Jason was there. As the ceremony proceeded, Jason held my hand as we listened to our pastor. His toast during the reception was heartfelt and sincere, just like him. We opened the dance floor together with Billy Joel's "Just the Way You Are." As the night faded on with photos and food, he found me during a quiet song and we danced. From the smile on his face, I knew he was having the best day ever. I leaned over and asked what his favorite part of the day was; he responded, "This."

And that's Jason. Honest, genuine, ever present in every moment. He was the perfect addition to our family then, and he has brought life and light into our world ever since. He is, without a doubt, the Best Brother.

I couldn't love you any better.
I love you just the way you are.

Billy Joel

"S" Stands for Superhero, Not Just Special

Marla Murasko
Plymouth, Indiana

This title describes our son so perfectly. From the moment he was born he was a fighter. He truly is our superhero. He's special and determined, as my blog, *Special and Determined*, is titled. He's special not because of his designer genes, but for the unconditional love he shows others. He is determined to make our lives, and the lives of those who know him, better.

He is truly an ambassador in our community for other children with Down syndrome that will follow in his footsteps. He is showing his school, his peers, and the community as a whole that children with disabilities can have a wonderful, quality life if only given the chance. They can thrive in school, make friends, play sports, and be seen as a valued member of their community.

Jacob has such an amazing group of friends who respect and care for him, watch over and support him, but more importantly include him. When I tell the parents how amazing their kids are for befriending Jacob, they respond back by telling me that having their child be friends with Jacob has made such an amazing and lasting impression in their child's life, which is so heartwarming to hear.

It's amazing what "inclusion" does not only for the child with special needs, but what it gives to other children. Inclusion in school and in sports allows young minds to learn about empathy and respect for others' differences. It helps foster friendships that would have not formed if typically developing children were not exposed to their peers with disabilities.

My husband and I agreed when Jacob was born that we would never let his disability discourage us from living as normal a life as we can. We love to travel as a family, go to sporting events and the movies, eat out, attend community events, and more! We enjoy living our life as a family with all its "special challenges."

When my son Jacob was born, I was having a difficult time working through all my emotions from his diagnosis. However, after much reflection and hearing the words that so many special needs families hear from others, "God had a reason for blessing you and your husband with your child," I improved. Those words are so difficult for any new parents to hear, as you feel your dreams of having a normal life are shattered. However, we can confidently say we know that reason. Our son is amazing and has filled our lives with so much love, happiness, and yes, some struggles, but we wouldn't change a thing. We are truly blessed!

I agree with this quote from Scott Hamilton: "The only disability in life is a bad attitude." Open up your hearts to others with differences, it's amazing what you can learn.

 You can follow the adventures of Jacob and his family at www.special-and-determined.com.

Great effort from great motives is the best definition of a happy life.

William Ellery Channing

Proud

Ilze van Deventer
Port Elizabeth, Eastern Cape, South Africa

The day Trace was born, it took me two days to come to terms. I didn't even need the blood test, I just knew from the first time I breastfed that there was a possibility that he may have Down syndrome. But once the tests came back I immediately told my friends and family. I made it my goal to talk openly about it, to learn as much as possible and join the Down Syndrome Association (never knowing I would be elected chairperson someday). I decided I would work harder than ever to make sure I could provide the care he needed, but most of all I needed to take care of myself so I could be strong for my kids. I started eating healthy, and running (I have since run two marathons, and train every morning at five a.m.). I knew that if I were confident and proud, my kids would be too.

Trace started walking at fourteen months. I couldn't believe it. Everyone told me it would take at least two years, so I was extremely emotional when I saw him take those first steps. But most of all I was proud of him, and I knew then that Trace would do very well despite everything else I had been told.

To Trace's cousins and his sister Ceri he is no different. They don't treat him unalike at all. However, some children realise that Trace is different and they'll ask Ceri why he can't speak. Ceri will say that he does speak and become surprised that the other kids can't understand him. Other kids gets irritated with him, mainly boys, because he can't play like them and his ways of doing things are different. For example, he may cling onto a ball if another boy would like to kick or throw it. Ceri will run to his rescue and she'll explain nicely to Trace what is required of him and tell the other child to not get irritated.

Trace continually makes me feel like a proud mother. At school he learns to choose tasks, colour in, paint, and clean up. He also learns about types of food, and to make healthy choices. Victory Kids is a fantastic school and he is very happy there. Trace likes to dress well, and he loves having a cool hairstyle! He is a big part of my family's and friends' lives, and I feel this is important in him having a life of opportunities. It's also extremely important that Trace is treated the same as his sister. I believe it helps Trace to reach the best of his abilities, which he always does!

There are tough days too, and we work through them, but mostly I am just so proud. I feel energetic, knowing that my kids and myself are here for each other to enjoy this life together.

Be content with what you have, rejoice in the way things are. When you realize there is nothing lacking, the whole world belongs to you.

Lao Tzu

David

Erik de Graaf and Marian de Graaf-Posthumus
Wanneperveen, The Netherlands

David de Graaf, our son with Down syndrome, is thirty-seven and lives a full life. Informing us where he has been and, even more importantly, what he has been doing on a particular day, however, is not his strongest point. To learn more about his experiences outside the family home, we gave him a digital camera way back in 2001. David enjoyed using it right away. Gradually, his output increased in quality, more and more focused in terms of being a picture rather than as a daily report for his parents.

The "breakthrough" came in the summer of 2003, when a photograph taken by him, mailed to a national TV station, appeared in the weather forecast on that particular day. From that time on, David very regularly produced 'weather pictures' for that same station, which are actually broadcast several times a year.

Over the years, David has used a sequence of digital cameras. Since 2018, he works with a semiprofessional mirrorless one equipped with an intermediate zoom. That means carrying one fairly large piece of equipment with a certain amount of automation. David determines the setting in relation to his surroundings. Daylight and outside, or inside? Next, he zooms in as far as he wants to, chooses where his focal point needs to be on his screen, levels his built-in-horizon marker, and shoots. The camera focuses and adjusts exposure accordingly. Twenty-first-century technology means a lot to him!

Because David currently holds a part-time job at the office of the Dutch Down Syndrome Foundation (SDS), his photographic abilities are often used during SDS activities. Examples are weekends for "new" parents with their kids, workshops, and dream nights at the zoo. In addition, he has produced material for several short film clips. He is also a volunteer waiter at the beautiful Sint Jansklooster nature reserve, where he uses his camera too.

In his free time, David loves festivals, his favorites being six special Thursdays in summer in the nearby town of Meppel. Since summer 2010, the local newspaper has used many pictures taken by him after every festival and through the rest of the year about the environment he lives in, traveling most of the time on his bicycle.

To keep himself in good shape, David loves fitness activities. It also serves as an important social opportunity.

In 2013, David had his first large photo exposition, featuring about thirty 60 x 40 cm dibonds. Many were to follow. A particular opportunity for David was to participate with three portraits in "Deep Down Arts" in Mexico. In the accompanying photograph, we see an enthusiastic David with Corona-style "haircut" next to one of his dibonds at his first exposition after the coronavirus lockdown in the Netherlands.

Now that David has blossomed into a photographer, we are fully aware of David's day-to-day whereabouts and experiences, and with or without his photographic achievements, we couldn't be prouder of his life.

Visit David's website, www.daviddefotograaf.nl, where you can follow along on his photo journeys.

If you hear a voice within you say "you cannot paint,"
then by all means paint, and that voice
will be silenced.

Vincent van Gogh

A Simple Hello

Jennifer Katz
Bronx, New York

I have mosaic Down syndrome. I was diagnosed in 1979, when I was nine years old. My parents realized that even from infancy that there was something . . . different about me. I was late reaching several milestones and had a few other issues. My parents decided to have me tested for chromosomal disorders at the NIH, at a friend's suggestion. Keep this in mind, as I continue.

I remember always feeling different. I found it easy to be friendly, but it was hard to make friends and even harder to keep friends. See, with Down syndrome, sometimes it's hard to understand boundaries. It took me a long time to learn them. But sometimes, I am capable saying just the right thing.

Fast-forward to 2008. I was married and had two wonderful young daughters. We were living in Dunwoody, Georgia, and I was dropping off my younger daughter to preschool in the neighborhood we were about to move to. I walked into the building and saw this little girl, bending over to fix her Velcro shoes. The first thing I noticed was her sleek, straight, super-shiny hair, up in pigtails. As she straightened, I saw her beautiful clear face. And then I noticed her eyes, a perfect almond shape. The round face, and the slight softness around her mouth.

The pieces fit together, and then . . . "Oh," I thought to myself. "She has Down syndrome! Just like me. She's soooo pretty, and it's clear this is her mom. I'll say hello!" I carefully approached the mom and said to her, "Oh my gosh, your daughter is so beautiful! Her hair is so shiny and pretty. And she looks to be my daughter's age. What's her name?"

The girl's mom looked—no, she gaped at me. Tears slowly welled up in her eyes. Choking back her emotion, she said, "You know, that's the first time someone noticed anything other than her disability to me." I was shocked, to put it mildly. How could anyone not notice her beauty first? Her hair, her poise, her smile, her outfit? Anything else other than that small detail. To me, it was unimportant. A describing feature, yes, but not as important as HERSELF—a young beautiful child at school, and it turned out she was in my daughter's classroom too! I told the mom briefly about me, and she was so amazed.

There was another little boy in her classroom whose younger sister also has Down syndrome! As it just so happens, Emory University has a genetics clinic in the area, so many families who have a child with Down syndrome live close by. I had no knowledge of this when we moved into the neighborhood. It didn't take long for me to be invited to meet the rest of the social group, since the mom of that first little girl spread the word about me; there were five families total. We got together very often to hang out, as families, at neighborhood/community events, at each other's houses, and at Mom's Night Out events. We still chat every so often even today. And it all started with a simple hello.

It takes only a minute to say hello, but it can make a big difference in someone's day!

Kate Summers

How Is Nik?

Maria Slater
Rusternburg, North West Province, South Africa

How is Nik? Nik is as he always is. He is singing "Thunder" by Imagine Dragons. I can hear his deep little voice echoing through our house. He's supposed to be singing an Afrikaans song to practice for his prize-giving concert. A storm brews as he obstinately refuses to perform the so-called laborious task of washing his hands before dinner.

At the prize giving, he is not much better. He is as stubborn as a tomato sauce stain on your best white shirt. You can beg and plead and pray, but if Nikolas doesn't want to listen, he most certainly won't. He didn't wear his little necktie or dance with his boisterous classmates at his prize giving. Instead, he gnawed on his fingers and attempted to hide behind his teacher. I felt slapped in the face by the universe. With Nik, progress is like slowly climbing up a steep, rocky mountain. Just when we've gotten somewhere, we step on some loose stones and tumble right back down to where we started. Or close to it, anyway. I left the prize giving with an empty feeling in the pit of my stomach because I dared to hope that the day would go better than the past six years or so of concerts with Nikolas.

Sometimes he copes better with certain activities, and the next day, he just . . . doesn't. And that's okay. To those of us who really know him, Nikolas is as unpredictable as a tropical storm. Unfortunately, people usually see him at the tempestuous times. You see his tantrum at the supermarket when we won't buy him six donuts. You see him refuse to eat anything that is not meat, pasta, or bathed in tomato sauce. You see his obstinate refusal to leave someone else's birthday candles alone. You see a minuscule drop of water in the torrent of rain that is Nikolas.

When someone asks me, "How is Nik?," it's like the sun peeking out after weeks of foggy weather. It's such a simple gesture, but it means the world to me. Because it's not comfortable to talk about disabilities, is it?

Maybe you believe that it's such a tragedy that he makes life at home so difficult for us. Well, you could not be more wrong. The real tragedy is not something that happened by chance to us, it's that people treat it as something to diplomatically tiptoe around like you're playing "The Floor Is Lava." It's that we're wrestling with the storm-spirit that is Nikolas, being soaked to the skin, and our souls are weary and the only thing louder than the thunder is the silence. The silence of friends and family who don't do something as simple as asking, "How is Nik?"

After the thunder, there is a long-awaited downpour of rain. This rain has brought a multitude of wonderful blessings. Nikolas chatters constantly, and I can only imagine the stories he tells. But I listen. I always listen. He can detect when someone has upset me, and even though he can't ask me about it, he's there. He makes me laugh so much that it just bursts uncontrollably out of me. He hugs me, whenever I ask for one. Now, as we sit down for dinner, he's only slightly uncooperative when it comes to washing his hands.

In the midst of a storm, the rainbow
reminds us that this will not last forever.

Anonymous

Just Waiting for His Daddy

Rob Snow
Medina, Ohio

I've spent the better part of the past six years hearing birth stories—sad, happy, funny, shocking, and all points in between. It seems the membership into our "club" requires a story, and never, in my opinion, is it a dull one. Most stories seem to have two parts whether the teller realizes it or not, and they are drastically different but equally important parts.

Part 1: Diagnosis

Our little guy, Henry, was born in March of 2009 and came out beautiful. I'm not one to always think that of children fresh from the womb. No, I need a hose and a towel. My wife does not need such things and finds beauty despite any gook. But Henry just had this undeniably pure face. It was so innocent, sweet, perfect.

The medical staff immediately began poking and prodding. Hours passed before our pediatrician walked into our lives. We had never met her and had chosen her randomly. She offered a few pleasantries and then examined Henry. "Well," she said, unemotionally. "I'm eighty percent sure your son has Down syndrome." As our hearts descended into our stomachs, she added, "But let me show you something." She opened her laptop to show us pictures of her daughter, who also had Down syndrome. We sat there with this new and seemingly terrible information looking at a very adorable little girl in pigtails playing soccer and laughing with her friends. For the next hours, this initially stoic, unemotional doctor walked us through Down syndrome 101 with as much patience and practicality as possible.

Part 2: Acceptance

Our doctor made us understand Down syndrome. She gave us advice and conveyed the joys a child with special needs can bring. She held back appropriately though, knowing that selling Down syndrome hours after the birth is difficult. She left and we were silent, hesitant to talk about things we weren't ready to discuss.

My wife asked me to go to the grocery store for snacks. The countless visitors we were so happily expecting prior to his birth, now seemed just short of a funeral procession we were about to endure. In my car, I thought it would be only right to have a chat with God. I wasn't incredibly religious at the time, and didn't often talk to God. It was a pretty one-sided conversation. "WHY US, GOD?" and "WHAT DID WE DO?" For some reason, though, my anger felt ostensible. The more I thought about my son and his perfect little face, the more my anger seemed wrong, like I was just going through the motions. Then I realized that this little boy, who had done nothing wrong, was just waiting for his daddy.

With that last thought, tears welling up, I looked up and asked God, "Why not us?" His response has come every day since then.

The heart of a father is the masterpiece of nature.

Antoine François Prévost

Madeline

Rosanne Stuart
Mount Ommaney, Australia

Last year we were at a fashion parade and Maddy said, "Mum, me, model." My little girl always loved being in the spotlight, and I knew at that moment she wanted to get up on the catwalk then and there. Of course this meant that I had to explain to her that she couldn't just climb up on the stage and model, which didn't go down well as you can imagine. But I also knew at that moment that my daughter was going to do something special.

After the parade, I explained to Maddy that if she wanted to be a model she would have to keep on the healthy eating schedule she had started earlier that year to keep up with her dance troupe. Nine months later, we were off to see a professional photographer. Maddy was super excited to do her first photo shoot. As for me, I was doing it to see if she would actually like doing a photo shoot; it is one thing to say you want to do something, but another to experience how it is done and decide you actually love it.

Well, she loved it, and when I previewed the photos the following week, I nearly fell out of my chair. I had always known my baby girl was cute, but in these photos she was stunning.

The next step was to see what other people thought of the photos of her in her bikini, which I posted on a closed Facebook page for parents with children living with Down syndrome. I wanted to know if the photos were too controversial; however, the feedback was phenomenal. People said the photos were in great taste and I should post them all over the world. So that is what I did. I created a public profile called *Madeline Stuart* on Facebook, and within a week her photos went viral. So many people said she was an inspiration. She gave people hope that their children living with Down syndrome would achieve anything they set their minds to.

Since then Maddy has walked the catwalk in New York for autoimmune awareness, has modelled at New York Fashion Week, and has become the face of a cosmetic company called Glossigirl, which makes her the first model with a disability to ever do this. She is now known as the first professional adult model with Down syndrome in the world and is actually supporting herself doing it. She also has a bag named after her called "The Madeline" by a handbag company called EverMaya.

Of course I believe this is just the beginning, and anyone that knows us also knows that this is not just about modelling, this is about changing the world, this is about creating inclusion, stopping discrimination, and breaking down those walls of confinement. Modelling is just the vehicle that is letting us do it. We want everyone to love and be loved; after all, that is all that truly matters.

It is time for parents to teach young people early on that in diversity there is beauty and there is strength.

Maya Angelou

Grandparents

Lois Schatz
Regina, Saskatchewan, Canada

"In case you haven't noticed, Kelsey isn't drinking." This is how we found out we were going to be grandparents for the first time. We were thrilled and instantly in love.

We were excited and awaited any updates on the pregnancy. In this day and age, it seems there are more ultrasounds and tests than back in my day—at around eleven weeks, my daughter-in-law and son had their first ultrasound. "They noticed something different with the nasal bone," they said. What does that mean? What can they see at eleven weeks? Now what? So many questions; it was a shock to us all. Then came the denial. But blood work and an amniocentesis confirmed Down syndrome.

Having been an NICU nurse for fourteen years, my mind went crazy. All the possible things that could be affected. The baby's heart, eyes, ears, tongue, and digestive system. I was frequently going to Dr. Google, and that wasn't a good thing. I was a mess. This is not what any of us planned. Now what?

The month of January flew by. The baby was growing great. The heart was fine. We all felt a bit better, but there was still something bugging me. During a car ride where we were stuck in traffic, I had a heart-to-heart with my daughter-in-law. As excited as I was about the baby, I needed to know if I could share the diagnosis with my family and friends. I felt I needed that permission and was so happy to receive it. Maybe I was being selfish, but I wanted all the shock and possible "I am so sorry" reactions out of the way. I received very few of those reactions, thank goodness. We talked about so much on that highway that evening, and it will be an hour I will never forget.

The pregnancy progressed. The nursery was decorated. Oma (that's me) made a cross-stitch picture for the nursery and bought baby clothes.

At thirty-two weeks, our precious Madeline Irene was born. She was a mighty 3 pounds, 11 ounces. She was perfect and a true rock star. Her NICU stay was needed only to grow and get older, and on her due date, she went home with some tube feeds but otherwise a perfect little baby.

We have no idea what our future holds, but no matter what, we have a beautiful grandbaby who will indeed grow up, and we as Oma and Opa will be with her all the way, doing what grandparents do best, and that is to love her with all our hearts.

Love is the greatest gift that one generation can leave to another.

Richard Garnett

Acknowledgments

First and foremost, this book has come to be because of all the wonderful contributors. Thank you for sharing your incredible stories from the heart. It has been an extraordinary journey collaborating with you. We are forever changed because of the passion and love poured into these pages. We also want to thank Pete Schiffer for believing in us, and the team at Schiffer Publishing for believing in this concept. Also, thank you to the many individuals who posted on Facebook and on blogs to spread the word about this endeavor. It is through your help that we met so many wonderful people and received the opportunity to share these amazing stories with the world. Mike Sullivan, spokesperson for Saving Down Syndrome, helped tremendously at the onset of our search for contributors. We are truly grateful for your help and support. Lastly, thank you to our families and friends, whom we love so much with all of our heart.

This book would not exist if it wasn't for my brilliant daughter Elizabeth Martins, the coeditor! She was the one who woke up the idea for these incredible stories. Thank you, Elizabeth, for helping this dream and vision to become a reality for the many people around the world who will hold it in their hands someday. Enjoy the journey—as we are—and may you all continue to discover many more reasons to smile.

Photo credits

Adele's Story: Modern Nest Photography. Sibling Bond: Chris Walden. Sisterhood is a Journey: Elizabeth Martins. Finding Joy: The Ng Sisters. It's About Abilities: Terri Rose. Jenna: E. & J. Reece & J. Guishard. No Limits: Debbie Lawrence. Welcome to Holland: Nancy Ney. Every Step: Jenn Ng Miu Leng. Blessing: Sara Ancich Photography. Left-Handed: Eamon Ward. Love of Life: The Gregoire Family. A Love Story: Alexandra Codina. This Is Happiness: Liza éverdal. Hope and Joy: Berkant Colak. A Gift: The Taylor Family. Hope: The Picture People. A Great Adventure: Roz Hull. Harvey: Lizzie Fernyhough Tye. A Letter to Myself: Chuck Douglas Photography. That Extra Something: Sandra Brossok. What a Difference a Day Makes: Sandra Brossok. Paths: Sue Bessell. My Precious Child: www.iStock.com/MissHibiscus. Each Other: Teresa Eaton. Love Each New Experience: Sarah Schwind, De Vita Photography. Blessed: Elna de Jager. Tandem: Julian Norman. Wonderful World: Joe Trombatore. Do You Need a Hug?: The Dittmar Family. Darling Natalia: Hayley Goleniowska @ Downs Side Up. No Boundaries: Leslie Spurlock Photography. Proms Are Fun: Ann Berube. Three-Point Shots: Earl Grow. Changing the World: Denise Russo. The Three-Winged Butterfly: Lindsey Kelley. Anything Can Happen, If You Let It: Mardra Sikora. Unexpected Trip to Holland: Shannon Banchero. Tena: Monika Jakic. Aimee: Natalie Connolly. Togetherness: Pina Rahill. Faith: Lisa Wajert. My Reason to Smile: The Eichhoff Family. Infinite: Samantha Ranwell. My Recipe for Perfection: Nicole Leavitt Photography. My Best Brother: Char Photography. "S" Stands for Superhero, Not Just Special: Angie Kain Photography. Proud: Liesel, Cor, and Arno. David: Marian de Graaf-Posthumus. Just Waiting for His Daddy: Terry Horner. Madeline: Rosanne Stuart. Grandparents: Schatz Family. Oh, Anna: Elizabeth Martins.

Pictured from left to right:
Elizabeth Martins, Anna Knauss & Andrea Knauss

Andrea Knauss, Elizabeth Martins, and Anna Knauss are from Philadelphia. Andrea works in the counseling field and loves to garden, Elizabeth works in publishing where she enjoys the written word, and Anna is a fashionista who enjoys performance arts. You can follow along with their journey and this book at Facebook.com/ReasonstoSmileBook.

Keith Harris is the father of Tim Harris, owner of Tim's Place, the first restaurant in the US owned by a person with Down syndrome.